A Bulgarian Refugee's Autobiography and
Provocative Approach to Business Success

FILOSOPHIES

by Fil Filipov
Simple things and hard work are
keystones to a winning business strategy

**NOTHING IS FOREVER
NISHTO NE E VECHNO**

e-mail: filosophies@aol.com

KHL
G·R·O·U·P

FIL FILIPOV: FILOSOPHIES

Author: Fil Filipov
The Construction History Makers Series – Filosophies
ISBN: 0-9530219-8-X
© KHL Group Ltd

Published in 2000 by KHL Group, Southfields,
Southview Road, Wadhurst, East Sussex TN5 6TP, UK
Tel: +44 (0)1892 784088 Fax: +44 (0)1892 784086
Web site: www.khl.com
Bookshop web site: www.khl-bookshop.com

Editor: Chuck Muth (Fensholt Marketing Communications, Inc.,
Brown Deer, WI, USA)
Sub-Editors: Paul Marsden, Rachel Ramsden
Production Manager: Saara Rootes
Publisher: Peter Watkinson
Printed and bound by: Hastings Printing Press, Hastings, East Sussex, UK
Design by: Conifer Design, Bexhill-on-Sea, East Sussex, UK

All rights reserved. No part of this work may be reproduced or transmitted in any form or by any means, electronic or mechanical, including photocopying, recording or by any information storage or retrieval system, without permission in writing from the publisher.

FIL FILIPOV: FILOSOPHIES

DEDICATION

This book is dedicated to my wife, Veronique, and my son, Steve, for their trust, support and total commitment to my beliefs, all of which have contributed immeasurably to my business success, family peace and enjoyment of life.

Fil Filipov,
September 2000.

Veronique and Fil Filipov.

FIL FILIPOV: FILOSOPHIES

Fil Filipov

1946   Born in Plovdiv, Bulgaria
1964   Escaped to Greece
1965   Emigrated to the USA
1965   Various menial jobs
1966   Started with International Harvester (IH) Chicago, Illinois
1972   Transferred to IH, Louisville, Kentucky
1979   Transferred to IH European Headquarters Paris, France
1980   IH Factory in Croix, France
1984   J.I. Case Company buys IH
1987   Case Poclain, Le Plessis, French Headquarters
1988   Case Construction Equipment Europe
1990   Tenneco Inc., Turkey
1993   Koehring Cranes & Excavators, Terex Corporation, Waverly, Iowa
1995   Terex Cranes, Inc. Conway, South Carolina
1999   Terex Cranes, Inc./Terex Lifting Chicago, Illinois

Fil Filipov, 10 years old.

Fil Filipov

FIL FILIPOV: FILOSOPHIES

INTRODUCTION

AN INTRODUCTION BY FIL FILIPOV

Ron DeFeo and I have worked together since 1993 in building the most diversified lifting company in the world. His leadership and support have been essential as we made the impossible, possible. I am sincerely grateful for the opportunities that were given to me and I particularly appreciate and thank Terex Corporation for allowing me to publish FILOSOPHIES.

How many times in life do people get a chance to succeed? For some, it is due to where they were born, who their parents are, what schools they attended, etc. The opportunities are numerous. For others, like Fil Filipov, most of the opportunities were self-determined. I am proud to have worked with Fil and to have participated in some of those opportunities.

We do not work with too many genuine characters in business, but Fil is one. Not because of his tremendous work ethic, or intensity, but rather because he shouldered responsibility so well. So many times I have met people who want the authority to make decisions, but shift responsibility for failure to others. Fil is willing to be responsible.

To work for Fil is difficult. But isn't real success tough? I would get plenty of complainers who couldn't stand the pressure and would let me know all the negatives. But we were on a mission, and Fil was our mission leader. The mission was to make our Lifting business a success — even where others would have given up. We succeeded. Some would say Fil is at his best in the worst of times. There is some truth to

FIL FILIPOV: FILOSOPHIES

this. But I would like to say that beneath the tough exterior is a man who does care about people, has integrity, is fair, and is a real thinker about business.

It would be far too superficial to see Fil as the tough operations guy he is. You cannot change where he has come from, but Fil Filipov is a complex and thoughtful leader who will always be welcome on my team.

Ron DeFeo
Chairman of the Board
Terex Corporation

INTRODUCTION

I want to acknowledge all the contributions, efforts and patience of the professionals that helped this novice to write this book. These include my ghost writer; Chuck Muth, who took over its editing when it appeared it was becoming like an baby elephant; and KHL Group, the publisher. I also want to particularly acknowledge what others say about Fil Filipov. The candid impressions of associates, employees, industry observers and friends and family are included to provide aother perspective on the road I have traveled.

I started thinking about this project three years ago (1997) and, uncharacteristically for me, it has taken longer that I ever thought. Bbut as they say, our lives are a work in progress. I sincerely hope the story of my journey benefits others.

In all my years in marketing communications, I have never had a client CEO get so involved in message and graphics. But this is Fil Filipov. He applies the same focus, stamina and involvement in this area as he devotes to every other function in his operations. Not surprisingly, this often leads to some unconventional - you could say, provocative - approaches. Again, this is Fil. This book is another example. He knew what he wanted to say. Hopefully, we have presented his message in an interesting and provocative a manner as the individual.

He didn't want a hard cover book because he didn't want it to be too expensive for others. Also it would not be consistent with everything he stands for. Not surprising.

Chuck Muth
Fensholt Marketing Communications, Inc.

FIL FILIPOV: FILOSOPHIES

CONTENTS

	PROLOGUE	1
I.	A REFUGEE'S STORY	5
II.	HARD WORK NEVER KILLED ANYONE	25
III.	NISHTO NE E VECHNO (NOTHING IS FOREVER)	43
IV.	A NEW BEGINNING – WAVERLY, IOWA	55
V.	SIMPLE, AVAILABLE AND COST EFFECTIVE	73
VI.	QUALITY AND TURNAROUNDS	87
VII.	BASIC BELIEFS – THE EIGHT M'S	111
VIII.	TAKING CHARGE AND LEADING	121
IX.	THEY CAN HANDLE THE TRUTH	127
X.	MY SUPPORT GROUP	135
XI.	SOFIA, BULGARIA REVISITED	145
	EPILOGUE	159
	APPENDIX Industry Observations Sample Action Plan - 100 Days Pain for Gain	161

FIL FILIPOV: FILOSOPHIES

PROLOGUE

ODE TO FIL

On reaching fifty, men deemed wise,
Stand back, reflect, Filosophize
On choices taken, decisions made
Crises handled, intuition obeyed.

Though some may tag him a Filistine
This man we gather here to wine.
Ladies swoon to his suave flattery
While colleagues wish he'd chose Filately.

The frightening temper, language fierce
A mere facade for friends to pierce?
Not always! For when he comes unglued
They wish he'd jammed in a Fillopian tube!

For all his charm, good looks and wit
Sexual prowess – or so it's writ.
A monogamous man, no Filanderer this,
As Veronique knew from their first kiss.

Friends don't Filter your feelings, forget your fears,
For a Filibuster won't happen here.
On to the next fifty, we all wish you well
The toast is Filipov, our great Friend Fil.

Written by Stuart Anderson on the occasion of Fil Filipov's 50th birthday, October 18, 1996.

FIL FILIPOV: FILOSOPHIES

PROLOGUE

Sitting in a comfortable Paris café with Veronique, his beloved French wife and constant companion, Fil Filipov has finally taken the time to relax. In just over a few weeks, he has visited customers and checked operations in nine different countries. It's the business trip from hell, unless you are Filipov. The frantic pace is a perfect fit for his energy level, a bottomless pit that drives his competitors crazy, and even causes those close to him to shake their heads – in envy and in dismay – because they know that's what he expects from them. Relaxation on a business trip? That's taboo for Filipov. But at least for this moment, he does what comes naturally for most people: He sits back and reflects.

His thoughts go back to more than 30 years ago. He's again in Europe, only this time the setting is a small prison cell in Greece. Exhausted and covered with river mud, it is remarkable that 17-year-old Filip Stoyanov Filipov is still alive, having dodged gunfire while fleeing his native Bulgaria the night before. Yet all he can think of is his mother and father who will continue to live under communism in Bulgaria. Did they understand why he left without telling them? Did they know why it was so important for him to have control of his own destiny, and that it wasn't possible under a regime that blocked prosperity much more effectively than it did border-skipping?

Seize control. Take risks. Achieve success. That's the story of Fil Filipov. He's been a winner at every level, from a broom-pusher in a Chicago factory to an expert in turning around struggling companies. All this without a college degree, formal management training or an adherence to popular management theories, just wits and constant determination. He believes in hard work, common sense, strict expense control and an absolute commitment to *Simple, Available and Cost Effective*.

Filipov started at International Harvester in 1966 as an hourly employee and moved to Louisville, Kentucky, in 1972 in a management position. Continuous promotions and his aggressive management style gave him the opportunity to manage businesses for International Harvester and its successor, J.I. Case Company, and then Tenneco, Inc. in its glory days. He subsequently made his more striking marks with Terex Corporation. During his 35-year career in the capital equipment sector, Filipov was instrumental in reviving under-performing operations in France, The United Kingdom, Germany, Italy and multiple situations in the United States.

Filosophies outlines Filipov's life journey and secrets to success. If you know Filipov, you will recognize his straightforward, at times caustic style. If you are not familiar with him, you may be taken aback by both his candor and his approach, but they are genuine – and they work. Driven in part by the harsh experiences of his youth, he is aggressive, if not, ruthless in the way he conducts business. And he makes no apologies.

"My business model is not complicated," he says. "Enter a known volume market. Produce a quality product but keep it simple enough to price it 20 percent below the competition. And most importantly, work your tail off – and demand that those who work for you do the same."

Filipov now oversees a $1 billion company, which he built in less than 10 years. Yet he has no administrative assistant and calls very few meetings. He views feel-good, consensus-building

PROLOGUE

management as a waste of time. He holds in disdain any profession whose function involves or infers unnecessary complexity, consultants, peddlers of computer software and engineers among them.

Told by Filipov, *Filosophies* is short and to the point. The first chapter offers a glimpse of his past: his upbringing in Bulgaria, his daring escape to freedom and his early years in the United States, when as a common worker he discovered and practiced the fundamental principles he now uses as a company leader. Without this history, readers could easily interpret Filipov as just another well-manicured executive who talks an impressive game, without experiencing true hardship or the reality of life on the factory floor.

In the remainder of the book, Filipov explains his "Filosophies," intermingled with examples from his personal and professional life. *Filosophies* is not a 'how-to-manual' nor is it a brag on how to become rich.

Rich he is not because his idea of rich is when you employ a full-time person to take care of your money.

It is a story of an individual who knows what it takes to recover from the depths and achieve phenomenal success. And at every step of the way, he remains true to his core beliefs. Surrounded by a few believers, Fil has been able to earn employee loyalty and dedication. He acknowledges that he is difficult to satisfy, but it is his firm belief that driven employees do not dwell on yesterday's accomplishments.

Filipov maintains there are three kinds of people in the world: Those who make things happen, those who watch things happen and those who don't have a clue as to what is happening. "Those who don't have a clue just want to collect a paycheck. Those who watch things happen cruise through life, and let someone else carry the load, only to bitch and moan when that person succeeds or fails. They want more money, a fancy title, but don't want to do a thing to earn it. Those who make things happen drive for results. They don't wake up thinking only of trying to impress their boss, but instead are committed to helping solve problems. They may be disliked, and seen by some as insensitive and hyperactive, but they jump to the front, grab the reins and get the job done. They are focused on the objectives, and are willing to do whatever it takes to achieve them. They are winners."

Reading it, there may be times when you think Filipov's expectations and methods are right on target, but simply unrealistic. That internal politics, such as a strong union shop or fear of losing good employees, makes becoming more demanding too risky if not impossible. Filipov doesn't buy that argument. If hard work causes some employees to leave, he says, good riddance. The only popularity contest that matters is the one with the customers. At the same time, as emphasized in his core operating principles, *The Eight M's*, he makes a plea for a more humane approach when reducing the headcount. He asks: "Why is a chief executive officer fired for poor results awarded a golden parachute worth millions of dollars, when workers laid off because of management's incompetence are given nothing?"

"Tough as they are, we must face the facts," Filipov says. "Modern business can only thrive by smashing feel-good solutions. No longer can executives ignore day-to-day operations, leaving the responsibility to middle managers who `tweak' rather than change, who prefer being friends to those they supervise rather than leaders who demand better results. Empowerment isn't what business is all about, in the past, now or 50 years from now. Unfortunately, whining has become akin to a national sport in many companies. It's time we take off our politically correct blinders and face reality."

I
A REFUGEE'S STORY

LEARN THE RULES SO YOU KNOW HOW TO BREAK THEM PROPERLY

You could say I was born at the wrong place at the wrong time. Plovdiv, the second largest city in Bulgaria with a quarter of a million people, was a city in distress. Once beautiful, it had turned dark and destitute, both physically and emotionally. Under Communist rule, personal prosperity was out of the question. There really was no reason to look forward to the future, unless you had the courage to try to leave.

My parents were village people, fiercely loyal to their family and incredibly hard working. My mother, who at 78 still lives in Bulgaria and looks after her great grandkids, cared for her two children and in her free time made what money she could as seamstress. My older sister passed away not long ago at the age of 55 from Addison disease.

My father was a tailor. When he was 14, he left home and walked 50 miles to work as a tailor's apprentice, an arrangement my grandfather had worked out with the tailor for a fee. When my grandfather needed to talk to my father about something important, such as a request for money, he too walked the entire 50 miles, sleeping by the side of the road when he grew tired.

Bulgaria then was a country of great contrast. Mostly rural,

Fil with his father and mother, Stoyan and Paza, during his first visit back to Bulgaria 20 years after escaping.

it suffered under the enormous weight of widespread poverty. Although it had thousands of miles of road, only 25 percent were paved. To put that into perspective, if that were the situation in the United States, only the highways would be paved – as soon as you reached the exit ramp, you would be on a dirt road. Jobs were scarce and wages for those lucky enough to gain employment were low. Many areas of the country had no plumbing or central heating.

Nowadays, about 80-85 percent of the roads are paved, though some of them are in bad condition, and a great proportion of them are highways. Some areas of the country, however, still have no plumbing or central heating.

Though proud, nearly a thousand years of oppression have forced the Bulgarians into a lifestyle of hard work for little gain that has, ultimately, made them stronger. To paraphrase Ernest Hemingway, oppression breaks everyone, and afterward many are stronger in the broken places. No more powerful truth could be said about the people of Bulgaria. Without going into too much unnecessary detail, I think a brief history of my ancestors will give you some perspective about my message. That history, as I recall it, can be best viewed as three distinct eras: the Golden Age of Bulgarian culture, the Ottoman oppression, and the Communist regime.

The first Bulgarian State was founded in 681 while Christianity was adopted by the Bulgarians in 864. The establishment of an autonomous Bulgarian church and the Slavonic alphabet created by the brothers Cyril and Methodius enabled Bulgarians to use their own language for state, civil and religious purposes. This created the foundation for the Golden Age of Bulgarian culture enjoyed under Tsar Simeon (893-927). Himself very well educated, Simeon spent 28 years ushering in cultural progress. Many schools were set up during this period and many of them produced masterpieces of Bulgarian literature and painting art.

In 1014 Bulgaria fell to the Byzantines and remained a vassal state for the next 170 years. In 1185 the two boyars Assen and Peter started a successful nationwide uprising against the Byzantines and the Second Bulgarian State was founded. Tsar Ivan Assen II (1218-1241) established a second Golden Age of the Bulgarian culture. Magnificent works were written at that time. Artisans and craftsmen filled the country with great works of art and magnificent architecture in the Byzantine style, including some of the most breathtaking churches in the world. Touching the Danube River, millions of acres of fertile land and majestic mountains made the perfect setting for a great culture.

This Golden Age also ended in violence. Hordes from the Ottoman Empire invaded the Balkans in 1362 and within the next 30 years had conquered all of Bulgaria. Over a period of more than 500 years, the invaders imposed a miserable life. Property and land were seized, meager earnings were heavily taxed, and any who refused to comply were immediately executed.

The year 1762 marked the beginning of the Bulgarian National Revival, a period probably even more important than the Golden Ages. It was characterized by a struggle for national and religious independence and gave rise to a great cultural upsurge. Trade contacts were established with the capitals of Europe. A series of uprisings against the Turks broke out in the 16th, 17th and 18th centuries but they all were unsuccessful. The cruel suppression of the April Uprising of 1876 aroused the indignation of all of Europe. Russia declared war on the Ottoman Empire and Bulgarian volunteers took part fighting side by side with the Russian troops. On March 3, 1878, the San Stafano Treaty was signed, by which a Bulgarian state was established. Under the Berlin Treaty, however, the country was torn into three parts and some of its territories remained under Turkish rule. On April 16, 1879, the first National Assembly convened at Veliko Turnovo to adopt a constitution and elect as monarch, Alexander Battenberg, a German prince. A revolutionary movement began which resulted in the unification of the Eastern Roumelia and the Principality of Bulgaria (the other two parts Bulgaria was divided into by the Berlin Treaty) on September 6, 1885. Bulgaria declared its full independence from Ottoman control on September 22, 1908.

Soon after, Bulgaria entered another period of conflict. First came the Balkan Wars, where Bulgaria joined with other Balkan countries to drive the Ottomans from Europe. Although successful, Bulgaria lost significant territory in post-war disputes. Hoping to gain back what we lost, we joined Germany in both World Wars, and instead of gaining land we lost more each time. Finally, Bulgaria was invaded by the Soviet union on September 8, 1944. The worst was yet to come.

On September 9, 1944, a resistance group coalition known

as the Fatherland Front assumed power. The coalition included Communists, Agrarians and Social Democrats and, although the Communists were in the minority, they were able to gain control of the key Justice and Interior ministries. The Front swept to victory in the November 1945 elections and the Communists undermined their coalition partners to gain control of the new Assembly – so consolidating their grab for power. They took immediate and brutal steps to seize power. Any person who was not a party member was removed from office, and many were killed or driven into prison camps. Personal freedoms were prohibited. Everyone's private property was seized for the convenience of the state.

Although my father eventually lost his business to the Communists, he always provided for us on a level just a little above the masses. Our family lived in a small home and most of our daily concerns centered around the basic necessities of food, clothing, shelter and fuel. At least we did not share our house with other families, but even at a level just above the masses, our home did not have a toilet inside, we had to go outside to a shed.

The majority of the houses, ours included, did not have baths or showers. We all had to use the public baths – you can imagine not every day. This is perhaps why the Bulgarians congratulated each other after a visit to the public baths. Our home had no central heating, no running water, no refrigerator or television set. I can still remember using a heated brick to keep warm under the blankets before falling asleep. Private car ownership was almost unheard of – I did not even have a bicycle.

The negative effects of communism threw our country further into decline. Poverty was already rampant, but it began to seep into even the most prestigious levels of society. Businesses, farmland and factories – essentially anything that could be used to create value – became state property. The party line was one of absolute compliance, regardless of how badly the people suffered. None of the government officials cared, and even though our country could still have been great, the mismanagement and apathy on the part of the Communists sent our lifestyle spiraling.

Most people's dreams hinged around visiting "the West." There's an old saying in Bulgaria which states that the reason someone dies with their eyes open is because they haven't seen America. After my escape, my father used to write letters to me, ending each one with, "Do you think I will die with my eyes open?" Many years later, my father fulfilled his dream when he traveled to my home in Louisville, Kentucky, for a visit. He died with his eyes closed a few years later at the age of 70.

I loathed communism. Everything about daily life was strictly controlled. Individuality was slowly and methodically forced out, religion was absolutely forbidden. In essence, the state demanded a monopoly not only on your lives, but on your dreams – and the evil of all evils was the total lack of *incentive*.

Under communist philosophy, all production is controlled by the government, including volume, quotas, prices, and when and where goods could be sold. In theory, this sounds like a good idea because the central authority can move supply to meet demand, and modify prices to make sure those who need something have access to it. In reality, however, it does not work because it is not efficient. Consumer demand does not affect quality or price very much when there is only one source of goods. Productivity is not high when there is no incentive. When you get the same wage for producing one or 100 tons of grain, you are likely to produce the lesser amount, if even that! Since the prices are set by the government, at values that do not reflect the actual cost of production, there is considerable waste in the system. When the basic essentials, food and shelter, are in short supply, the incessant propaganda rings hallow – it does not matter what the government says, the tough times tell you differently and the credibility of the Communists is destroyed.

A REFUGEE'S STORY

Equally destructive is the monopoly on privilege. In Bulgaria, the higher you rose in the Communist Party, the more privileges you enjoyed. Only children of party members could attend specific colleges, for example, a fact that greatly influenced my decision to escape. I was an ambitious child and a very good student, with constant drive to be first in everything. Although I wanted to attend the university, I was blocked by the unwritten rules of hard-line communism. You see, grades had no value; performance didn't matter; attitude counted for nothing. All that counted was the political clout that came from embracing communism and joining the party, something that neither my father nor I ever considered. That was a difficult blow for me, since I truly wanted to be a mechanical engineer. I loved mathematics. I enjoyed the precision of getting things right the first time by laying them out carefully. But in this environment, it was not to be. Knowing in advance that college was out of the question, I attended a technical school for textile manufacturing at the tender age of 12.

Textiles were one of the great exports of Bulgaria. Unfortunately, a textile factory can be an extremely dirty, noisy and irritating environment. The Bulgarian textile plants of the 1960s were close to the kind of facilities that American industry outlawed in the early part of the 20th century – completely unsafe, and with no regard for worker's health or welfare.

In early 1964, my frustration reached its limit, and not surprisingly, I couldn't keep my thoughts to myself. I mumbled something about how badly the government was mismanaging my country and how things were not so rosy. I knew it was a stupid thing to do, but it was the truth, and I have always been long on telling the truth no matter what the cost. I was called into a police station and subjected to interrogation in a scene reminiscent of a third-rate Mafia movie. A massive, balding man kicked me around the room, pouring out Marxist philosophy and cursing me as an anti-social troublemaker. He extolled the virtues of communism, the "one true form of people's government" and "the best thing to put bread on the table." The only problem was that bread was rarely on my table, or anyone else's, for that matter.

Around that same time, I saw the Academy-Award winning movie "Room at the Top," the story of a young man who claws his way to success from a tough environment littered with obstacles. He was determined to succeed no matter what it took. The film's powerful sense of adventure and capitalist thinking fueled my desire to leave Bulgaria. I am sure others who saw it felt the same way. Even to this day, I can't believe the censor bureau allowed this film to be shown in Bulgaria. Was it the fact that after he reached his objective in a rich society he was unhappy, or did they just slip up? At that time the majority of the films were produced by the Soviet Union and, of course, in each one of them the Russians always won. They typically had a horse and a train. From time to time I remember we were allowed to see some French comedies.

The confrontation and the movie crystallized my resolve. Although I returned to the plant with its hazardous conditions and demoralized work force, I quietly started to hash out plans for my escape. You have to understand in a country where every other person was a government spy, it was wise to keep all thoughts of fleeing for a better life to yourself. I did not even tell my parents.

I had a distant cousin who lived near the Bulgarian-Greek-Turkish border. My plan was to visit him, after which I would take a little side trip to the West. While waiting for the travel permits, which should have taken about a month, I mentioned to

*GREAT LOVE AND GREAT ACHIEVEMENTS
INVOLVE GREAT RISK*

Filip Filipov's Request to Travel to Border document.

my best friend that I was leaving, and he insisted on coming along. A distant acquaintance of ours happened to overhear the conversation and threatened to tell the police if he wasn't included. Papers were required for everything in Bulgaria, including special permission to go close to a border town.

On May 17, 1964, the three of us rode a train from the center of Bulgaria, two-and-a-half hours, to the border. It's an odd feeling, looking out of the window and watching your homeland pass by, realizing that you may never see it again. All those days I spent enjoying the simple things – things that didn't cost much money, like climbing the mountains and hills and wandering through the woods – all those things would be gone. There is a Bible verse that talks about "putting away childish things," and that is certainly what we were doing.

When we arrived at my cousin's house, we discovered that he was not about to stay behind. So there we were, four young men at the height of the Cold War, two years after the construction of the Berlin Wall, standing at the border between Bulgaria and Greece, between the stronghold of communism and the birthplace of free thinking. After a couple of false starts, we took off in the rain.

We learned in eight seconds what most people never grasp in a lifetime: Making the decision and taking the first step is simple; following it up can be hell, but it's the only way to succeed. Gunfire erupted on all sides, accompanied by flares and troops on horseback. To complete our escape, we had to cross a wide river and make it through murky, swampy terrain. One minute we were sprinting across the uncertain ground of a river island, the next swimming for our lives, not wanting to know whether those slapping sounds were our hands groping for freedom or rifle rounds pelting the water. Finally, after breaking all records for running in mud, the four of us made it into what we thought was Greece.

We saw an elderly man tending a herd of cows, but when greeting him in Greek, his reply was in pure Bulgarian, "Where are you guys going?" We figured the Communists had set up a

A REFUGEE'S STORY

double border to fool escapees, so we immediately started running again. Finally, when we saw a car's license plate that was not Bulgarian, we knew we were in the right country.

At first, we weren't sure escape was the right decision. The Greek police arrested us as potential spies, separated us and threw us into prison. In those days, the number of Communist spies coming out of Bulgaria and other border nations, under the guise of "refugees seeking political asylum," was significant, and the Greeks – along with the CIA, I am sure – had to be careful. I now understand their concern, but when I was on the receiving end, it was not comfortable. We were not allowed to see each other. We were kept in prison cells and interrogated daily. They asked us the same questions over and over again, watching to see if we might slip up and say something that would give us

Three of the escapees (left to right), Fil Filipov, Bozidar Talaganov and Dimitar Manolov (since deceased) in a refugee camp in Greece. This photo was recovered after being confiscated by the Communist authorities who numbered the individuals for identification purposes. The fourth escapee (Nickola Grozev) is not in the picture.

Greek refugee camp, 1964. Fil Filipov is to the immediate left of exiled Bulgarian King Simeon (center in suit) and her majesty Margarita.

away as a KGB agent, or worse, a member of the Bulgarian Secret Police, one of the most hated and strong-armed organizations in history. Our captors couldn't be too careful.

After the Greek authorities were satisfied that we were not spies, and having refused to become a spy and go back into Bulgaria, we were transferred to a refugee camp for persons seeking political asylum. While it was not the most pleasant place I've ever been, it had a certain charm, and it gave me an opportunity to learn new cultures and languages – something that would serve me well all my life. I learned Greek, along with some Spanish and a number of other languages, at least well enough to get around. After a few months, we were asked to identify three countries where we would like to emigrate. Our selections, for various reasons, were France, Belgium and the United States. In Belgium we thought we could go to the mines, work hard and become rich. We selected France because of our dreams to date and marry pretty French women, an aspiration I achieved later in life. The United States was everyone's dream. In all honesty, though, my friends were somewhat hesitant about the United States, where the likelihood for personal success – and failure – was all up to you. (The Communist propaganda had apparently made an impact, after all.) Upon reflection, however, and after France and Belgium had granted us visas, we decided to go to the States. We understood it was the greatest place in the world, the land of opportunity where hard work could lead to success and wealth.

We flew to New York City, economy class I am sure, but I do not remember. It was the first time any of us had been on an airplane.

I arrived in America on January 6, 1965, the day before the Orthodox Christmas, with a bag containing just a few possessions. Representatives of the World Church Organization (WCO) picked us up at the airport and we were given a room at boarding house in Harlem along with $40 and encouragement to look for work. Then we were on our own.

New York City was breathtaking – the buildings, all the traffic and expressways. Then the magnitude of it all hit me. Walking around Rockefeller Center a little later, I had to be the most unhappy person around. Seeing all the stores and holiday lights and me in my thin moccasin shoes and no money, no job, doubt and fear began to creep in. I had to think, was it the right move coming to America? I was alone, a refugee without a friend I could call on, but I reminded myself of why I came here in the first place.

Meanwhile, the Bulgarian government was offering my parents little information about my whereabouts, and what they did share were lies and rumors. As I mentioned earlier, I did not tell my parents that I was leaving – my biggest fear was that they would talk me out of it. In any case, who wants to listen when they are between 15 and 25, and I was only seventeen.

Capitalizing on my parents' worries, the Secret Police circulated stories about finding the bodies of several teenagers who were shot to death during an escape. Years later we learned how ridiculous these tales were; that most of the border soldiers were actually sympathetic to the escapees, sometimes related, and often fired errant shots on purpose.

As a classmate, Nasko Tchervenkov, recalled later, after my escape all the students were called into a general meeting and were told that I had left Bulgaria. I was called an enemy of the state, a spy, etc. The students who were my friends were called in one by one by the school management. They were criticized for not being vigilant enough to see what I intended to do and to inform them about that. They were sad and tense times, but fortunately they stopped after about 10 days. Months after my escape, I sent a letter to Nasko and in it I briefly explained to him what had pushed me to leave Bulgaria. I said the main reason was not hatred for Bulgaria, but a desire for a fuller life. A few days after receiving the letter he was called in by the State Security office. The plain clothed officer asked him if he had heard from me. He immediately associated his question with the letter. They already knew about it. When he told them about the letter they said that it would not be advisable to continue corresponding with me and ordered him to turn the letter over.

Although I know my parents ultimately agreed with my decision to escape, I am sorry for the grief it caused them and others. Because of it, my father lost his job and finished his career as a common laborer. My mother was continually oppressed at work. Several distant relatives also suffered through interrogation. A day or two after my escape, students at my school gathered to throw rocks at a crude image of me, calling me a traitor. Yes, I was a traitor to communism, and I was proud of it.

Finding a job in New York City at that time wasn't easy, especially when the person could speak no English and had absolutely no knowledge of the area. After about two weeks, I was wondering whether pure capitalism was the smartest move. Nobody seemed to care whether we lived or died; nobody seemed to even notice that we were there. This was a big change from my home country, where personal relationships define a lot more of the culture than they do in the United States. Since none of us could find jobs anywhere, we went back to the WCO and received one-way train tickets to Chicago, where we had heard there was plenty of work and other Bulgarian refugees. To the best of my recollection, this is the one and only time I have taken a train in the United States. I often ask myself, why aren't trains used more in the United States?

Arrangements were made for someone to meet us in Chicago, but the person never showed up. After spending two nights and a day in the cold, uncomfortable train station, a Bulgarian immigrant group in the area got us out of the station and into the homes of a couple of Bulgarian-American families.

Although it was a huge relief to have some stability, I was still determined to find work and get out on my own. I used the Greek I had learned at the refugee camp to get dishwasher's job at a local Greek restaurant. The job was not glamorous. The pay was minimal. But with it, I took another small but important step forward. I have studied some of the most influential people in history, and discovered that they were willing to do whatever it took to succeed – step by step, always moving forward.

Yes, I may have been born in the wrong place at the wrong time. Overrun by the Ottomans, then treated like chattel by the Communist regime that followed, depression among the residents of Bulgaria was common. Many of the people simply gave up. I was not about to let that happen. Maybe it was my youth. Maybe it was the values instilled by my nose-to-the-grindstone parents. Most likely, it was a combination of factors, including my simple, steadfast belief that success is a matter of effort and a few well-thought-out risks. If I was willing to do what it takes, I felt I could achieve almost anything.

It is worth noting that of the four young men who fled Bulgaria on that gray, rainy afternoon, not all of us took advantage of the opportunity. The one acquaintance who said he would squeal to the authorities if we did not take him along, died young in America, penniless from gambling. It illustrates my point about taking the lead and making things happen, about not relying on others or sheer luck. He didn't, and paid for it with his life. May he rest in peace.

WHAT OTHERS SAY...

Nasko Tchervenkov
Classmate from Bulgaria
Plovdiv, Bulgaria
It is not easy to describe in a few words a man with such a checkered life as Fil Filipov. I have known him for many years as a grand person and a good and generous friend. In the last 10 years I have grown to know Fil not only as a man, but also as an industrialist. He is a real "architect" of the metal-processing and engineering industry. He has had great success in the reorganization and refinement of many industrial enterprises all over the world. Because of him, I was able to see some of his achievements in Europe for which I am very grateful. I would also like to thank him for presenting me with the opportunity, if only with some small projects, to become a part of his precise and creative world of industry. Fil Filipov is sparing of words, modest and very rich in worldly and industrial knowledge. I wish him a long life and every success in the tough world of metal.

A REFUGEE'S STORY

Uri Toudjarov
Sales Manager
Terex Cranes
Waverly, Iowa USA
Fil Filipov inspires, motivates, leads and drives people to achieve results beyond their belief. His energy, charisma and "joie de vivre" make him larger than life. Most people have heroes that they never get a chance to meet or talk to. I am privileged to have a hero who I consider a friend for life. Fil has the ability to see into the future. With an extreme sense of intuition, he thinks 10 steps ahead of everyone else. For the past 25 years, I have listened to and followed Fil's "filosophies." Fil Filipov is an innovator who has revolutionized the lifting industry forever.

Bozidar (Bob) Talaganov
(The one who helped me swim the river.)
Owner of Transportation Company
Chicago, Illinois USA
I was born about a mile away from Fil's childhood home and have known him longer than anyone else. Even his parents have not spent as much time with him as I have.

On the day in early 1964, when he broke the news to me that he was planning to escape from Bulgaria into Greece, we were picking snails for some pocket money. There was no way my friend was leaving without me. The rest of the story of our escape, I am sure, has already been told.

Let me assure you that few people have endured, or should I say enjoyed, a relationship like ours. We never allowed a little dispute to injure our great friendship and God knows we have gone through some hard times.

Fil's father was a well-respected tailor who taught his young son how to run a sewing machine and actually to sew a pair of pants. The Communists did not permit any influence from the West and blue jeans were not sold in Bulgaria. No matter, Fil used his ingenuity and skill to create for his friend his own version of blue jeans. It was my first encounter with western style.

Fil was an entrepreneur even then. Personal things were hard to obtain and I remember him making some special neckties, his own design, and selling them to the graduating students. It would not surprise me if he still carries in his "accounts receivable" the money that people owed him when we left. Little did we know then that he would some day be known for "Simple, Available and Cost Effective" in a completely different industry.

In 1965, about a dozen of us, all Bulgarian refugees, started working for International Harvester Company in Chicago. But only Fil stuck it out. The rest of us were looking to become rich very fast and moved on to what we thought were more promising fields. Fil has stayed with the construction equipment industry for more than 25 years, and made a very successful career out of it.

His persistence is well known. He has taken his career path and life to levels most refugees never reach, but he never forgets where he came from and he is always there to help a friend.

I was the one who taught him how to swim in the dirty river running through our home town. I helped him swim the river during our escape. In return, he is the one who has helped me swim in the business world.

My hope is that young people coming to this country do not make some of the mistakes that we did in our early days. Fil's initiative to write this book about our experiences and his success will benefit other young people, including my children.

He drove everybody crazy the same way – we can do better tomorrow than we did yesterday-and if I sound like him after 40 years of friendship I am proud of it. We are all proud of his accomplishments.

A REFUGEE'S STORY

Marko I. Rachev
President, Marken Tool Co., Inc.
Mundelein, Illinois USA

I had the opportunity to meet Fil in Greece in 1964. He had just escaped from Bulgaria as I had before him. Even at a young age, he had that magnetism with people and leadership quality, and was eager to conquer the world. And indeed he has, with the lifting industry where his superb business sense has kept him ahead of the competition. He took the challenge and changed the lifting industry around the world. I am proud to be his friend.

FIL FILIPOV: FILOSOPHIES

II
HARD WORK NEVER KILLED ANYONE

I didn't leave Bulgaria to become a playboy. With business success my goal, I realized I had to work hard. It was that simple. Hard work requires focus, and keeps you focused. It prevents you from getting drawn into office politics and gossip. Most importantly, it produces results.

How wrong are so many people who think that all you have to do is wake up and pick the dollar bills from the trees. America is not at all what they think it is! A great opportunity and hard work is what America is all about.

As I mentioned earlier, my first job in the United States was washing dishes. Strange how many people would find shame in starting there, but I had no problem with it at all. I worked hard and did whatever the boss asked of me, although, in all honesty, the work was not that difficult. I was never one to sit still. Within a few weeks, a position was available with a company that packed electronic parts, such as television tubes. It looked like a golden opportunity to influence my own destiny.

There were no limits to the number of hours I could work, so I put in 12-15 hours a day, six days a week, and 10 hours on Sunday. I did everything the job required and everything else that was available to be done. Then one day my boss started walking around the shop, giving out raises within earshot of everyone. Most people were getting raises of between 20 and 30 cents per hour. When he approached me, he said I would be getting an extra nickel (5 cents) per hour. I was furious. Here I was, working harder and smarter than most people in the place, and getting only a fraction of their increase. If that's all he could give me, I didn't need to work there. I threw the box I was packing into a corner and told him in no uncertain terms that I could do without his raise – and his job. Of course, he got me into the office and tried to talk me into coming back with a much higher increase, but you can never go back in those situations: The glass was broken. Once again, I had to stand up for myself. Nothing is forever.

I have always believed that honesty and hard work deserve a reward, and anytime I find myself in a situation where the rewards are not commensurate with the work being done, I get out. Staying would be hypocrisy. I try hard to be consistent in my dealings with everyone, to be honest with myself and others, and to stick to my promises. This is not always easy, especially when there is easy money to be made by changing stripes. That kind of success never lasts, however, and eventually you will lose friends and fail to be able to influence anyone, because they will have no faith in you. Credibility is essential in life and in business. Hypocrisy destroys credibility and arrogance kills.

Hard work has rewarded me, if by nothing other than the results obtained and the freedom to work. On the flip side, if we don't reward our most productive employees, the competitor will, and we will suffer for it. Luck has nothing to do with success, only hard, smart, honest work and careful timing. Although I am a superstitious person, I believe that luck doesn't really exist – it's where hard work meets opportunity. In a country like America, where freedom offers a multitude of opportunities, luck does not even enter the picture. Timing is everything.

It's sad that so many people look for the easy way and end up falling in love with things that drag them down: drugs, excessive drinking, overeating, smoking, dependent relationships and the ultimate diversion, television. They look for the quick fix to give their life some meaning, only to discover it doesn't help at all. I remember when giving up smoking, cold turkey, after puffing two to three packs a day for over 30 years. It was not easy, but after careful consideration of what I was doing to myself and the time I was wasting, I just quit – end of story. Most people don't think they have that kind of strength, but when something else is more important, you will be motivated to change. Even to this day, people give credit to my wife for my quitting smoking – they are wrong, I can testify to it.

Something that truly bothers me about America is our slavery to credit. So many people forget that credit is money we haven't worked for yet, so by going into debt we obligate ourselves to hard work after the fact. Trouble is, people never repay the bills by doing the hard work it implies. Rather, some take the easy way out and file for personal bankruptcy. I for one am thankful that the government is cracking down on this practice. It may sound cruel, but people need to be held accountable for their foolishness and lack of self-control.

Throughout history, entire towns have been built around a single industry or corporation, with the employer providing everything. People moved to these towns, lured by the promise of high wages and plenty of overtime. Arriving there, they found high wages, but also discovered their employer had a monopoly on survival itself. Homes and living space had to be purchased from the employer at far above market value. Food and other necessary goods were purchased in the company store at excessive prices. Using these methods, corporations retrieved much of their payroll costs, effectively paying their workers a starvation wage. A number of American folk songs of the late 19th and early 20th centuries carry the line, "I owe my soul to the company store." Thanks to legislation and the advance of communication and transportation systems, these practices have been largely set aside.

Today, however, credit has become a new and effective method of retrieving payroll. Banks and lending institutions have become the "wage recovery" branch of many major corporations, encouraging consumers to spend their salary far in advance to acquire things they really don't need. These recovered wages are then used as startup capital for businesses, or to make large loans to existing companies.

Unnecessary debt destroys. It's ironic that the renowned entrepreneur P.T. Barnum – who once said, "There's a sucker born every minute" – warned people to avoid debt at all costs. A few chapters away, I will talk about how negative cash flow kills a business. The same is true for individuals, and credit often leads to negative cash flow. People willingly mortgage many years of future income for the pleasure of having something right now, and it usually comes back to haunt them.

I do not mean to say that there should be no credit, because when it is used properly, it is an extremely valuable tool. But there's such a simple way around it: Just wait until money is put away to buy the things you'll really enjoy. Then, when you are surprised with a true emergency, you won't have to borrow money from friends to make the trip – you can use your credit card appropriately. Everyone who knows how to do business competitively understands when and where to go into debt. When used carelessly, however, it amounts to gambling with the future, and is based on the naive or arrogant notion that current income and ability to generate income will always be there. This attitude can be a killer, because nothing is forever. I try to remember that capitalism is all about making it on your own, converting personal hard work into real, meaningful gain and a better quality of life. Lending companies, advertisers and labor unions have distorted what hard work means, and as a result, they give people the impression that mediocrity and spending money as fast as you can make it should be rewarded. That's just not so.

HARD WORK *WILL* BE REWARDED

I have tried to encourage a different approach to success. In my organizations, compensation is based on who sticks with the program, who stays late to get the job done, who puts in the extra effort. If you achieve more, you will be paid more. We might not be friends, our interactions might be unpredictable, but if you get the job done, I will reward you, period. What people say means very little to me. What they do, means everything. It's all about demonstrating competence. In fact, demonstrating competence is what kept me out of the poorhouse after I told my boss to stuff it at the packing company.

After leaving in a rage that day, I was on my usual eight-mile walk home (I didn't have a car in those days) when I noticed a "Help Wanted" sign outside a machine shop. My English wasn't all that good in those days, but I knew how to fill out an application. It seemed to be a small and friendly shop, so I carried the sign inside and found the owner. When he asked what I knew, my limited English prevented me from explaining the technical school training I had received in Bulgaria. Then an idea hit me: I would show him what I could do. The owner understood my request, gave me a pair of coveralls, a blueprint and a piece of steel.

What an opportunity! I went right to work. The piece I was directed to make was not a simple item, so it took about six hours to complete using various machines around the shop. That was good, because it gave me the chance to demonstrate that I knew several different machining techniques. Never once in that six hours did I let up in the least. I wanted him to know how valuable this job was to me, so I worked as fast as I could while maintaining a high standard of workmanship. When the part was finished, I presented it to the owner, and he remarked on how quickly and accurately the piece had been made. I got the job. I didn't bother to ask about the pay. Working for someone who appreciates hard work and real competence is worth much more, and it just didn't matter to me. I knew he would do right by me. Besides, the employers who really appreciate hard work are the ones that usually bring pleasant surprises, as I discovered only a few weeks later.

Since I was in the habit of working 12-hour days, I just continued it in this new job. Plenty of work was available. I loved the idea that I was getting ahead by my own hand. When I received my first check, it looked like a mistake, because the rate was $3.50 an hour – 50 percent more than what I had made in my previous position. From my perspective, I became a rich man. I was raking in money and not spending very much, putting it aside and looking to the future. After about 30 days, I happened to notice that my paycheck was too high. I calculated the gross and it came to $4 per hour. I went directly to the owner and told him there was a mistake. When questioned, he simply responded, "Oh, I forgot to tell you – I gave you a raise." At that point, I gave up any childhood notions about the failings of capitalism.

On that note, it's disheartening to see so many Americans fail to live up or, worse yet, even try to live up to their potential. I know an individual who's approaching 40 and has everything he needs to succeed. He has a great job with one of the top computer firms in the country. If he were to put in the effort, he could be promoted within a year and probably end up running the company. He's also involved in an outside project that could set him up for life.

I called him the other day and he was watching television, lamenting that he needed to call his father to borrow a few hundred bucks to get by. He had all kinds of schemes to bring in money, but not doing anything about them. Worse yet, the rest of the family had the same lackadaisical attitude he did, watching television and not lifting a finger to contribute. His car had broken down, so he was renting some expensive sedan because his wife wouldn't stand for a smaller model and wouldn't even consider taking the bus. He was even doing most of the housework. Here he was with an earning potential in the millions, doing the housework because his family doesn't want to miss their favorite TV shows. He had no plan. He had no goals, short or long term. He was putting in the minimum necessary effort his boss, his family and himself would allow.

I really let him have it. I told him he needed to wake up and take advantage of his talent. He needed to put an end to wasteful spending, turn off the tube and confront, rather than avoid, his problems. I volunteered to help him crawl out of the mud, but only if he did exactly as I said. That meant getting to the office early (instead of showing up after 9 a.m.) and immediately working on his most profitable project; riding the bus; keeping his focus on building a career; and letting someone else do a share of the menial work for a change. Basically, I had to push him past his laziness – and I pushed hard.

I spoke to him a while later, and discovered that he was starting to do well. Even he was surprised, because by his new standards he was barely breaking a sweat. Employees around him were as lazy as he used to be, so his willingness to stay late and solve the difficult, uninteresting problems made him instantly popular with the higher-ups. Walk through any business on a Saturday or Sunday and see who's there. They are the people who are and will always be successful – if, that is, they continue to put in the effort.

Although I really enjoyed working at the machine shop, I realized that capitalism is all about reaching for the next level. My roommate at the time was an artist who was sketching in Old Town Chicago and documenting the birth of the hippies. That was an experience in itself. I never joined the hippie movement, although I was right in the middle of it. I also was a rebel, but I didn't let non-conformity drive me to the extreme, because it gives the rules of resisting as much control over us as if we followed them. It was clear, however, that this resistance was going to stick around, so my roommate and I hatched a plan. We started buying pictures and frames, and together opened an art studio. I started working nights at the machine shop so I could run the studio during the day, and my friend covered it at night. Because many of our customers didn't have much of a normal schedule, we often stayed open until 2 a.m. I really enjoyed that arrangement, but unfortunately the machine shop couldn't find insurance to keep the night shift going. So I took a third-shift job at a capital goods manufacturer. Jobs at that time were plentiful. In fact, companies were paying finder's fees for referrals – even for broom pushers – if people stayed on the job for a month. This is how it was that I came to take the job that really launched my career.

In 1966, I started out sweeping the floors at International Harvester Company in Chicago, then a major manufacturer of agricultural and construction machinery. From the perspectives of work and pay, it wasn't as good as my previous job, but it gave me the time I needed to run the art studio during the day. Two steps forward and one backwards is always one step forward. I worked very hard at three jobs, 20 hours a day, seven days a week, holding onto my dream of making it to the top. I managed the studio during the afternoon, making picture frames, helping customers and creating clay masks for ceramic molds. When 11 p.m. rolled around, I went right to work at International Harvester, then on 26th and California Avenue. After finishing the night shift, I sold vacuum cleaners door-to-door, taking brooms as trade-ins. I remember many times waiting at the front door, watching the housewife run out the back to find somebody's broom, or hurry off to the local market to buy one. It was a trade-in trick, but people did not know it.

It didn't take long before my diligence at International Harvester got me in trouble with the union. Back then in that particular industry, the work was incredibly greasy and dirty. After your shift, you didn't think of getting in your car and driving straight home. Instead, the company had showers so that line employees could clean up before leaving the plant. In the shower at the end of a shift, the union steward approached me and, through an interpreter, complained that I was working too hard and needed to slack off. Boy, did that burn me up. Here I was, having escaped communism and run from gunfire to get the chance to make my own way in the world, and now I was being told to start being lazy so that everyone else could be lazy, too. I told him right away I wasn't going to change. I was coming from the biggest Union there was – the Soviet Union – and he was not going to tell me what to do. There was an element of risk in doing that, because the unions in those days had devious ways of making people cooperate. As it turned out, though, he never bothered me again, and I worked as hard as I wanted.

I didn't just push the broom, either. While eating lunch and taking breaks, I watched the machine operators to absorb all that they did and how they did it. One evening while cleaning an area, I heard the supervisor complaining because an operator didn't show up for work and production was lagging. Another opportunity, courtesy of hard work and paying attention. No problem, I told him. I volunteered to run the machine, and after a short trial found myself with a new job. At that point it was clear that manufacturing was going to be an excellent career for me, so I dropped my other interests and started working 12-hour shifts at the plant. Learning one new machine led to the next one, and eventually I started to know the entire production line very well. I kept at it, producing as much quality product as I possibly could. Within a couple of years, I earned a promotion to third-shift group leader. Never one to let up, I continued putting in my best effort every day, now with 60 people to motivate and teach about hard work – something I've found is more rewarding than almost anything in life.

This was my first observation of how not to run an operation. Management was very weak and was oblivious to the abuses and problems that ultimately caused it to fail – the place was dirty, had too much inventory, had too many chiefs and not enough indians, and management did not seem to care.

When the Chicago plant closed it came as no surprise to me, and the company moved me to Louisville, Kentucky, as a management trainee. I liked Louisville, and the management program was a tremendous opportunity. Eager to learn, I put in every possible minute at the office, doing my best to learn the business inside-out. Step by step, I kept chipping away at my dream of making it to the top, capturing 11 promotions in seven years. By 1978, only 15 years after my escape, I was supervising 700 people on an assembly line producing 60 tractors per day. My work hours were typically from 5:30 a.m. until 9 at night, and I loved every minute of it.

After one promotion, the area I had left started having trouble and I was asked to come back. It was something of a step backwards, so I returned on one condition: If I met the necessary objectives and productivity went up, I would be offered an overseas assignment. I was deeply interested in moving to Europe, so again I put hard work to the test: long hours, smart moves and concentrated focus on the objectives. After 15 months the job was done, and the company lived up to its commitment. With great expectations, I moved to Paris, France, as a project manager, supervising a major European investment.

The European way of life was something I dearly loved and

HARD WORK NEVER KILLED ANYONE

1980 in Paris with my children, Nadia and Steve.

the exposure to other cultures and languages was wonderful for my two young children. I have come to believe that learning languages develops other skills as well, and this was certainly true with my children. Unfortunately, it was the beginning of the end for my first marriage. Compared to the States, many parts of Europe fall short when it comes to amenities, and that hardly pleased my first wife. In spite of my marital troubles, the work went extremely well and, for me, the lifestyle was pleasant. Again, I quickly earned a reputation for hard work and focused effort designed to deliver results. The timing was right for my move.

WHEN YOU LOSE, DON'T LOSE THE LESSON

After being in Paris for about a year, it became apparent that an overhaul was needed in a factory located in Croix which is in the far northern part of France, near the Belgian border. Learning over the years that there is tremendous opportunity in chaos, I decided one more time to step backwards – into the factory – and turn things around. It was a monumental undertaking: starting with over 1,000 people, reducing the headcount by more than 50 percent and completely restructuring the operation to make it profitable. Many things needed to be changed, but mostly there were lots of people on the payroll who really weren't contributing to the business. This was probably my first strong confirmation that staying in the firing line pays off.

At times, I really was on the firing line. At one point, I was held hostage in my own office for 36 hours by workers who demanded that I stop the downsizing. This was a difficult time, because I do not arbitrarily let people go. Cuts are always made based on who is needed for the remaining tasks and to look after the company's interests. Fortunately, I am not an easily intimidated individual. Once the strike was over and the labor force stabilized things progressed quite well. The organization became "lean and mean." There was no bureaucracy, no useless activity and no nonsense. Although it resisted, the union leadership knew the score. Previous management did not make things clear, the plants were not producing enough to meet customer demand and the operations were not profitable. Even though some jobs had to be cut, the doors stayed open, something that wouldn't have happened had I not taken drastic measures. Today, many of those same union leaders would say that in spite of the rough spots, this was one of the best periods in the history of the facility. That factory is still producing the largest share of its product in Europe at competitive prices, and investments have reached a record high.

In November 1987, the city of Croix, France, presented me with a gold medal for keeping the factory open. With cost always on my mind, during the acceptance speech I remarked that, if my wishes come true, one half of the city's present government would not be here so taxes would be reduced.

A colleague who had been there 30 years observed this was the first time he saw a medal presented to someone for reducing employment by 50 percent. But the factory was never closed.

Keeping a failing plant from closing has always been my objective in tough situations, even if it means alienating some people. That can be tough when unions are involved because they do not contribute to the well-being of the employees, employment or future growth. In all honesty, I do not find that unions are really all that dangerous, nor are they the ones who really run the companies. The majority of the time, strong unions exist due to weak management. When trying to get something done in any given operation, the strength of the union isn't the most important thing. What is crucial is being honest and straightforward in both word and deed, and to refrain from playing politics. Both sides must be clear about what they want to achieve and be willing to work hard at reaching a compromise. Yes, you do have to play a little politics, and at times losing the battle to win the war is more important, but even when it's two steps forward and one step back, it has to be a one step forward solution. If you're not taking any steps forward, do whatever is necessary to get the place profitable again, or just close the doors. Remember, by standing still, we risk going backwards. There is no excuse, union or not, for allowing an unprofitable operation to continue. Any knowledgeable union leader knows that it's in the best interest of everyone to keep the place going. In most cases the problem is not the work force, but a small group of middle management protecting their jobs.

Dealing in different countries with different traditions and different unions, you need to understand them to be successful in negotiations. I always go in with an open mind and an understanding of what their tradition is. In France, one has to be aware that labor unions are very political, but less than 15 percent of the people carry union cards. Many people who really don't know France are very negative about the French labor force. But in fact, it is a French weakness to be more negative than positive. Having worked in this environment for a long time and knowing their tradition and language has always helped me to successfully deal with not only the labor force, but local authorities that in many cases are necessary for the business to be successful. In no other country that I have worked are the local authorities more involved and helpful.

On the contrary, dealing in the German environment, I have discovered that the strength of German union federations and the positive attitude of the work councils toward the business objectives are very different than any other country in the world. When used properly, work councils in Germany contribute greatly to the success of the operation. I can remember a group that I had to negotiate with in 1989 concerning the closure of a factory in Düsseldorf and how hard they negotiated. Yet when we reached an agreement after many, many hours, how fair and disciplined they were in co-operating to do the most undesirable task in the closing of the factory.

Dealings with labor unions in Latin countries requires openness and detailed explanations for the actions to be taken. In most cases during my dealing with unions in Italy and Spain, I found that the representatives of the labor federation that were dispatched to the particular location for a specific meeting were like business consultants with a lot of authority. Again, my dealings in those countries have been very successful due to my understanding of their culture and tradition.

In any case, one problem is common to all countries, middle and upper management's unwillingness to do things differently, to recognize the failures, and their resistance to move in new directions. They act like a dog with a bone – won't eat it, but don't want to give it up either. This is why, when I take over an operation, one of my first steps is to identify and eliminate the resisting elements.

In over 15 years experience in the international, or should I say global business environment, I sometimes like to put the management of several different countries into a conference room and experiment with the nature of each nationality. Put in French, German, English and American managers and if you propose something new, the receptions are very predictable.

> The Germans will immediately say, "No, we don't agree."
> The French will argue and make charts, but will do it.
> The English will promise to do it but will do it their way.
> The Americans will tell you, "Let us show you how we do it in the USA."

Fortunately, unions and much of what they represent is on the way out. In the beginning, they were needed to deal with truly unfair and unjust labor practices, but lately they have become simply an organized way for only a few workers to whine about having to do an honest day's work. One of the biggest problems I have is their insistence that decisions about downsizing be based on seniority instead of performance. This system rewards people for being around a long time, so working hard the first four or five years you are with a company entitles you to relax for the rest of your career and be promoted based strictly on coming to work every day. There is no merit in such a system – none whatsoever. If you cannot continue to perform at an acceptable level, retire or find a new job, period. As global competition presses prices down, companies have no choice but to reduce costs and increase productivity or go out of business. Faced with those choices, the unions either back down or disappear, usually leaving their members stranded.

As you've probably guessed by now, I am a strong individual. Consequently, the unions that exist in my plants are just the opposite. That includes the facilities I have managed in Germany, where unions have protected the world's highest standard of living. They are honest and dogged in their fight, but used to getting their way. Even in Germany, the principle applies that weak management leads to strong unions, and vice versa. Without strength at the helm, unions overrun the company and hard work goes out the window. For example, in Germany there are six weeks legal vacation, while in France there are five. These extended vacations, which are common in Europe, actually make sense because it should help lower absenteeism. But a strong union called IG METALL is really the one that fought management to get the six weeks. It is very important for executives to stand up to this kind of nonsense and get a fair deal for everyone. Look at Caterpillar, which diligently fought the United Auto Workers for a fair contract, and U.S. President Reagan, who refused to give in to the Air Traffic Controllers. And, of course, think of the people in eastern Europe, who stood up to the most formidable and nastiest "Union" of all – the Soviet Union.

AS YOU SOW...

Hard work, with focused effort on desired goals, never killed anyone. It gives birth to results and prosperity. As a manager, remember that diligent, intelligent effort must be rewarded, or you risk losing your most valuable assets. As an employee, if hard work doesn't mean much to your boss or doesn't seem to make a difference, you have some serious thinking to do. It might be frightening to walk away from a sure thing, but you need to move forward, which may mean moving out – one step back, two steps forward. Above all else, avoid the trap of using credit. Capitalism is not about going into debt, but about converting your hard work into maximum gain and avoiding the ladder of mediocrity which so many seem content to climb.

FIL FILIPOV: FILOSOPHIES

III
NISHTO NE E VECHNO
(NOTHING IS FOREVER)

On August 22, 1991, the headline in the New Orleans *Times-Picayune* read, "They Chose Freedom." The article underneath referred to the collapse of the former Soviet Union, which ultimately fell not because it was overpowered by democracy, but because it could not provide for its citizens in a world that was rapidly leaving it behind. I remember telling some classmates that "Nishto ne e vechno" and they would say "Only communism is." Well, now they know, "Nishto ne e vechno."

From my perspective, the former Soviet Union never understood the wisdom of the saying, "Nothing is forever." I have always felt that success means recognizing reality and meeting things where they are, not where we would like them to be. It's easy to get caught up in a system, taking it for granted until it wipes you out. Constantly question everything, and if it isn't working, change it as quickly as possible. Those thousands of small, day-to-day adjustments may not seem like much, but collectively they make a huge difference. Find things that can be done better, and change them. It is the only way. That is why I knew the collapse of the Soviet Union was only a matter of time. Its government was blinded by a system – a system which never worked in the first place. Not only did the government refuse to change, its people lacked both the freedom and the motivation to change their own situations for the better.

Before I was born, my father opened his own tailor shop, practicing the skills he had developed as an apprentice. He was diligent, content and earning enough to support his family. Then came the Communists. As they assumed power, everything in the shop – all the equipment, material and hard work – became state property. My father could continue to work in the shop, but he no longer owned it, and he could no longer profit from it. All money was destined for the state, to be distributed as the government saw fit. For their efforts, my father and his employees received small salaries. The incentive that drove them to do everything necessary to make a profit, particularly to work hard, was gone. My father couldn't stand working under such an arrangement, so to save his pride, he left the business. At the age of 11, I watched my family start from scratch. My father had enough guts to sell his house in the village, move back to the city and start over by working for a large corporation to save face.

Little did I know that I was learning a fundamental principle that would serve me well for many years: Nothing is forever. As my father realized, the most important thing to do is to maintain your freedom as much as you can, which often means hard work, sacrifice, a willingness to do whatever it takes.

Someone once said, "If you continue to do what you've always done, you'll always get what you've always gotten." That is absolutely true. Things change constantly, and we must change with them if we want to survive; you must be really good at change if you want to thrive. Even the largest, most successful companies can quickly go under if they fail to acknowledge change.

I've taken advantage of this fact more than once to wipe out competition several times my size. This didn't happen because of additional capital, or better leverage or a more empowered workforce. Nor did it come about because of things I'd read in popular management books. David-conquers-Goliath acquisitions are made possible by just one thing: understanding the importance of meeting the customers where they are, as they are, with what they really need.

"All well and good," you might say, "This sounds wonderful for a cutthroat niche market, but what about the real world?" You may wonder why re-engineering has hung on so long, with so much industry applause, if that isn't the right approach to take. Well, it has to do with people's misguided resistance to change. There are far too many systems, such as re-engineering, and people cling to them with all their might. Why can't they learn to trust their own intuition? Yes, we will make mistakes, but how else can one gain the wisdom and maturity to make good decisions? Before we know it, we begin to trust the system and attribute all our successes to it. This can cause us to get confused about cause and effect. If we think about it that way, it's easy to understand how modern business has become mixed up over re-engineering. When inflation is the rule, when there are too many dollars chasing too few goods, companies can distract themselves with all kinds of unnecessary and unproductive activities and still make enough profit to feel good about what they've accomplished.

Re-engineering and empowerment came along at just such a time: Firms were hiring and customers were buying like crazy. Since products were largely selling themselves, middle management had plenty of time on its hands. Out of a need to feel busy, perhaps, or maybe just a desire to justify someone's job, re-engineering and "empowered management" were born. There were all kinds of experimental ideas, too, but the worst of them probably had to do with eliminating management and running the business with teams.

It's wonderful to have people working together, but the idea that they have to spend a lot of time learning to like each other is nonsense. If I'm a professional and focus on the objectives, I can literally hate the guy I'm working with and still be extremely productive. The old rules about never mixing business with pleasure, and leaving your personal prejudices and tastes at home need to be resurrected. Spending energy so that everybody can be buddies and hopefully work well together is fruitless, and doesn't contribute much to the bottom line. But in a boom time, nobody cares.

Unfortunately, businesses see results and incorrectly attribute them to re-engineering, team management and other internal mechanics, rather than the excellent economic environment. If anything, these fancy techniques and over-hyped procedures just keep the managers out of the way while the people in the trenches sell the product. Like the savage who touches the radio antenna and claims magical powers, many companies have become enamored of their procedures and lost sight of common sense. And, like any experience which borders on the mystical, they only see paradise in their future. In its essence, this attitude constitutes arrogance, and that's dangerous. No matter how large the share of the market, no matter how well things are going, we must stay on top of things and adjust to achieve even more. Even in times of prosperity, it's all right to be dissatisfied. It is one of the major reasons capitalism has worked, and socialism has crumbled. As Americans there is always another level of success to which we can strive to achieve – a better-paying job, a larger house, a nicer car – and we have the freedom to try to achieve it, within the law. The people of the Soviet Union were limited to what they could achieve, and lacked the freedom to even reach that level.

It is sad that re-engineering has become an end in itself for many once powerful companies. A well-known business proverb states that a camel is a horse built by committee. Nowhere does this adage bear itself out so well as in the team empowered, con-

NISHTO NE E VECHNO (NOTHING IS FOREVER)

sensus driven halls of re-engineered corporate America. In a rush to embrace new buzz words like "global management" and "favorable market spaces," with casual disdain for the ultimate customer as someone to be educated, corporate decision makers struggle with totally incompatible ideas in a vain and costly attempt to bring everyone's opinion into the mix. The results? Massive downsizing, sooner or later.

If we place a goldfish in a bowl of water and slowly turn up the flame, the goldfish will just sit there and die. But if you tap on the bowl, the fish will jump and escape. It seems as if modern corporations are so convinced of their own longevity and invincibility that they don't sense the fire under the bowl. Teams assigned by management are delegated with responsibilities that they are not qualified to undertake and do not have the authority to complete. They stumble around in the dark, re-discovering things that managers already know and focusing on making a good impression, instead of getting the job done. Worse yet, companies turn the profit/loss controls over to each team or business unit, pitting them against each other in a war that usually depletes energy and dilutes revenue. I looked at the detailed annual report of one corporation and discovered that its information technology department had a phenomenal year, showing a profit of 148 percent, while all other areas showed slight losses. The problem? That information technology department only received money from other divisions within the same company. If this kind of internal money laundering is not stopped, it becomes a cancer that eats away at the organization. In this instance, unless management breaks out of the hypnotic trance of empowerment and taps on the glass, the business will just sit there and collapse, never realizing what happened. That's where I come in – I tap on the bowl and get things moving before it's too late.

Intense global competition has already turned up the heat, dropping prices and lowering margins. In the last few years, more and more barriers to international trade have fallen, and countries once in the second tier have come to the front. In the years to come, there will be more adjustments to pricing structures and the way purchasing power is determined. Auctioning on the Internet will come very close to doing what we had done already! The customer will be king – creating a very competitive marketplace.

Personally, I think inflation is very unlikely for at least the next 20 years, since there's plenty of money in 401K plans and other savings sources that is going to be invested. The stock market continues to provide major funding and remains a source of encouragement in a global economy. Many people seem to be concerned about the market collapsing under its own weight, but we have to remember that there is plenty of cash available to keep it floating. Barring some major catastrophe, the upward trend in the market should continue for quite some time. While adjustments that stem from a global economy ruled by exchange rates will have the most powerful impact on business, they will not be the only impacts. There will also be good, old-fashioned, down-and-dirty competition that will force cost reductions. The watchwords of the current climate are elimination of waste, reduction of corporate bureaucracy and the pruning of unnecessary administration, and, quite clearly, productivity improvements in each sector of each of the major economies.

More interesting is the array of new players. Russia and Eastern bloc nations have grown weary of being bullied around. A disorganized group of European nations, the European Union (EU), also figures in the equation, although I don't expect the organization will function very well for many years to come. Not all of the member nations are happy with the currency conversion that will take place, moving from individual national currencies to the Euro. As we already know, I am not at all a supporter of consolidations – it has never worked. In the midst of all this confusion, the new and deconsolidated Eastern Europe may very well be the next force for least cost production, prosperous economic conditions and future growth. Its people are proud, and will quickly recognize that they can do what other parts of Europe have done in the last 50 years, catch up to the American standard of living and create their own economic niche.

Still, with all the capital available and favorable interest rates, the world markets will continue to grow. And who will grow with it? Only those companies with the highest productivity and lowest cost. Companies must face up to things as they really are, whether that be in the market or in the workforce. We must not give up our freedom to make things happen the way we want them to happen, and be prepared to change as necessary to maintain that freedom, rather than trying to make the world fit our perceptions. We must adjust constantly as we get new information or as things change. These changes will not always be large or obvious or feel like tremendous decisions, but we must treat them as such. Depending on a pat method or a recommended system will not solve the problems.

Remember that insanity is often defined as doing the same thing over and over again and expecting a different result. I control my destiny by always being aware of where I am compared to where I want to be, and making small, continuous adjustments in any and every thing that needs changing. Nothing ... absolutely nothing ... is forever.

WHAT OTHERS SAY...

Kiril & Violina Vasilev
Personal Friends
Plovdiv, Bulgaria

Violina Vasileva
My husband Kiril and I are from Plovdiv – the home city of Fil Filipov.

FIL FILIPOV: FILOSOPHIES

We met Fil in 1986 accidentally, as is usually the case with all good things in life. Since then we have been joined together by a sincere friendship, one that I could hardly imagine my life being without. Now looking back on the memories, I realize it was all predetermined.

It took incredible courage for that 17-year-old boy to escape from Bulgaria and to radically change his life. The success he has achieved since then comes as no surprise.

My husband and I have been engaged in our own business since 1990 and Fil, always available as a concerned and kind-hearted friend, has readily provided help and appropriate advice about our work. Without realizing it, I try to emulate him. This is not easy at all since he has that inborn talent to be a leader.

I eagerly look forward to his book being published in Bulgarian so that I can have a course book about life and business.

Everybody knows Fil the businessman, the leader, but I know Fil is a loving and devoted son as well, who cares deeply about his family in Bulgaria. I know he loves coming to Bulgaria.

We wish him good health and energy to continue to make his way in business and in life. He knows that we love him very much and he can always rely on us. I hope that his motto, Nothing Is Forever, is not valid for our friendship. I am counting on the fact that every rule has its exceptions.

Kiril Vasilev

To the most successful Bulgarian in industry.

Nothing is forever – It could be that in your favorite motto lies the basis for your success. The motto speaks for itself, prompts you to act, move forward in good times and not accept the bad.

You left Bulgaria not because you did not have love for it, or because the Communists were in power and it was too early to know of politics, but because their philosophy did not give your searching character the opportunity to develop and find a better life.

They thought they would last forever, but they failed. Their phi-

losophy was stagnant, and you realized that and knew that early on.

You would not have achieved what you have in business if it had not been for your drive for something better, leaving behind what had already transpired.

I know, my friend, not everything has always been OK for these 36 years, but that same early drive has given you the strength to overcome the disappointments.

I am sure many people have experienced and prospered from your dynamic development philosophy. I am equally certain there are others who could not endure your dynamics and are no longer present in your life.

Some may say that you have been too strict with them, that you have been a dictator. Do not worry because it is unyielding dictatorship in the right and constructive direction that leaves a trace in history. Everybody remembers Caesar, nobody remembers who came before or after him.

Others try to adapt to your dynamics, and those people you help. I have never met anyone so willing to help those who are ready to do the right thing.

And we, your friends, are by your side.

We continue to try to learn more or do it your way. Sometimes it does not work so we try again. We are aware that we can always receive your good advice and assistance.

Fil, I know that nothing lasts forever. But it is my fervent wish that our friendship endures, certainly at least as long we are alive.

Good luck, my friend!

Alain Brusselle
Assistant to the Mayor of
Wasquehal, France
Fil Filipov had to express himself about his perception of human beings, his ideas, and his strong opinion of how companies should be managed. I hope with "Filosophies" he opens his heart and lets us have it all.

FIL FILIPOV: FILOSOPHIES

I had the pleasure of meeting Fil in the early '80s. The factory – then International Harvester France – was to be closed. He did not go along with the idea and wanted local authorities to help him keep it open. Tough restructuring and layoffs followed: "You can't make an omelet without breaking eggs," he would say. Even the controversial union leader who used to call Fil "the social cowboy" recognized that the man worked very hard and was respected by the workforce. His hard work, the local authority's help, the union's cooperation and the efforts of the employees kept the plant from closing. It is still open and Fil Filipov proved it could be done!

Ten years later – Fil gone for five – some smart headquarter people of Case Corporation decided the Croix-Wasquehal factory should be closed. On behalf of the unions and the Mayor of Wasquehal, Gerard Vignoble, I contacted Fil in Waverly, Iowa, asking him one more time for help. We all believed he was the only one able to do it – keep the Croix-Wasquehal factory open and produce quality products. He had told us that, "When you dance with the bear, it's not you who decides when to stop, but the bear." Nineteen months later – one more time – with his help, the top management was convinced and kept the factory in the group. Today the factory still employs 400 people and is a part of a big new group called CNH. Who knows – someday we may have to call on him again. As the saying goes, there are never two times without a third.

It is my pleasure to contribute to "Filosophies" and to talk about Fil Filipov. A strong bond built during the tough times has created a warm friendship and mutual respect within our families. You will not believe it, but we take some vacations together. Even when I steer the boat he wants to tell me how to do it – but that's Fil. We have not always agreed in our discussions and views, but I must admit that he is almost always right. He knows how to adapt, but never gives up on what he considers as essential and always finds the words and the way to convince.

Fil and Veronique will always be welcome in our home and I may

NISHTO NE E VECHNO (NOTHING IS FOREVER)

even continue to be his skipper. I will soon be getting into the mode of "doing nothing but doing it well." Who knows, one day he may...do nothing and do it well. Will his "Filosophies" allow it? Remember Fil, Nishto ne e vechno.

Fil and Veronique Filipov, Violina and Kiril Vasilev, Michelle and Alain Brusselle on vacation in Greece, in 2000.

FIL FILIPOV: FILOSOPHIES

IV
A NEW BEGINNING – WAVERLY, IOWA

In the fall of 1992, Ron DeFeo, who had just joined Terex Corporation's Heavy Equipment Group, called and asked me to go to Waverly, Iowa to assess and provide a report on the operations of Koehring Cranes & Excavators. I had met Ron in 1989 when he joined Case and came to Europe. He knew me as a hard-nosed manufacturing guy and my input would be part of the decision to either fix the plant or close it.

Koehring Cranes & Excavators was acquired by Terex in 1987 and while it had a rich history of accomplishments with strong brand recognition, recent performance had been dismal.

I was not excited about going to such a rural area, to a very small company with sales less than $100 million, large losses every year and all kinds of products from dirt to mainstream goods. Nevertheless, after a couple of months, Ron DeFeo convinced me to visit. I submitted a comprehensive report of what I found and recommendations for corrective action. He responded by promising me a piece of the action: If the situation at the factory was unresolvable, they would give me ownership of a product line. Obviously, they had figured out what made me tick, which is my love for the operations side of business. I accepted and in January 1993, my wife and I went to Chicago, rented a car and drove to Waverly, Iowa. As we drove, she kept asking where it was, because it wasn't on the map. A small town of only 9,000 people, it has a certain charm, right down to the main street. Frankly though, from Paris, France, to Waverly looked like several steps backwards.

Rustic or not, it was a very tough start. Initially there as a consultant, I realized that the plant didn't need to be closed. There was tremendous potential in the place, which could be capitalized on by restructuring the product lines, facility and cost framework. In short, it was a viable business when the organization was trimmed down to size. I made them a counter-proposal: Go ahead and restructure the business to recover profitability. With only seven or eight people in the general office and no headquarters bureaucracy, Terex quickly approved the plan – no cash required. I went right to work.

Leon Deutsch, then financial officer for Koehring Cranes & Excavators and now a Senior Vice President of Terex Lifting recalls:

Fil Filipov was here bright and early the day after New Years with a plan, divide and conquer. Little did the people in Waverly know that this meant everything from supplies and inventory to people and products.

At this point in his career Filipov only had manufacturing experience. He had never been responsible for all other related business functions. Maybe this would be a new beginning for both Filipov and the Waverly plant.

Outside sales and marketing people continued to say how bad the market was and that that was the reason why they couldn't sell. This did not register with Filipov. His only thought was that if this plant could build simple, available and cost effective products, they would sell.

Everything was done in small pieces. Filipov had a vision of making Waverly into an assembly plant to reduce the lead time to make a crane from four months to 10 days. Nothing was impossible to him if you set your mind to it and really believed

A NEW BEGINNING – WAVERLY, IOWA

that it could be done. We quickly learned never to tell him, "It can't be done." In the beginning he was all alone with no one on his side. The people in Waverly had seen so many saviors come and go that this was just another guy in the chain. What we didn't know was that he was a firm believer that timing was everything. He firmly believes that politicians, sports people and business people all make the same mistake of not knowing when to keep going and when to quit. We soon found out it was his time to make things happen.

The plan started with the complete separation of cranes from dirt machines. There was so much inventory on hand that the only thing we could afford to do was to build machines from what we had on hand and try to sell them. The sales people said the machines could not be sold. The response from Filipov was everything has a price and if you have a good product at a reasonable price it will sell.

Within a few days after the start of the New Year, the excavator inventory started to move from the main plant to a satellite plant and people were assigned to specific tasks. The vision Filipov had was shared with only a few people, or maybe it would be better to say only a few people understood the vision. Things started to happen in small ways. After all, Filipov was just a consultant and current management did not agree with proposed changes. They also did not believe in hard work and in fact never showed up on Saturday. The ship was sinking because there was no captain. Things needed to be changed. Filipov did not wait for authority to be given, he took charge.

In March 1993, Fil Filipov became the 24th president of the Waverly facility in the past 23 or 24 years. It was time for things to happen. No more games or time to think about things. Decisions were made and actions were taken.

In his remarks to Koehring employees when he took over in March, 1993, he made it perfectly clear what was ahead – the pain for gain that would be experienced in the next 100 days, the kind of people he felt were necessary to change things for the better, what had to be done and some of the ways it was going to get done. And he closed with words of encouragement to enlist everyone's support and extraordinary effort.

In ongoing messages, he communicated where we were at ... what kind of effort was required...how to make improvements ... how the turnaround was progressing. Always candid, blunt and soliciting/demanding cooperation and unforgiving implementation.

Cash was king and the business was run on a cash basis. If it took cash and we didn't have enough, there was always another way. Factory supplies were used up and not replaced until such time we had exhausted all alternatives. The lights were turned off in all areas where people were not working. The heat in the plant and offices was cut back to save cost. All expenses were approved in advance by Filipov himself.

When he assumed control, the marketing manager was away in Florida and Filipov ordered him back to Waverly. Another salesman was down in Acapulco, selling who knows what. Digging further, Filipov found sales people who had given their company cars to their wives and were using taxis for their own transportation. He had to wonder how anyone could sell under these circumstances and, needless to say, things changed immediately.

When vendors would not supply components because of our bad reputation, we would visit the suppliers ourselves. This often meant leaving at 4 a.m. to drive to Milwaukee or Chicago, seeing three suppliers and returning home at midnight. The next day started again at the normal 6 a.m. When asked why he went to work so early the next day, Fil's response was, perception. He said, "The workers on the floor don't know what I did yesterday, they only know that the pressure is off if I'm not here before they are in the morning." It is amazing to work for a man who never missed a day because of illness. When he caught a cold everyone thought he would take a day off. They were disappointed.

Housekeeping at Waverly, deplorable on day one, was improved on a daily basis. The word was you cannot build good products in a dirty shop. There was no tolerance for people not cleaning up after themselves or having unclean employee restrooms.

The work day started at 6 a.m. or before and lasted until 10 p.m. There were many times when Filipov was in the plant 24 hours a day. There was no time to stop – things had to get done. The few customers we had wanted products on time and in good working order. There was no backlog at the beginning of the month and we had to rely on orders received during the month for results. The pressure was on the few remaining sales people to deliver. People were classified as either making things or selling things. If you did not fit into one of these two classes your job was in jeopardy. Many people participated and the ones that didn't were left behind.

In early spring, Easter Sunday to be exact, Filipov asked me how many people I thought were eating Sunday dinner and depending upon a paycheck from the Terex Waverly plant. The quick estimate was approximately 2,000. With this in mind he seemed even more committed to fixing the place rather than just making changes.

Buildings were torn down eliminating places for people to put things and avoid working. There were union problems as work rules were enforced and the contract was challenged to meet delivery schedules. The message was out: Filipov was not going to go away. It might be better to join him than to fight him. The place and the results were starting to turn around.

By summer good things were happening as a result of our increased involvement with the few customers we had, but there were not enough orders to generate the sales volume required to reduce product cost. Operating expenses had been reduced drastically, housekeeping was getting better and there was at least some glimmer of hope.

Craig Lichty, then Koehring Cranes & Excavators Marketing Manager, now Senior vice President, Sales & Marketing, Terex Lifting (thanks to his wife, Dana, who advised him to stick with this crazy man) looks back:
At that point, we had equipment for sale which we offered at the best possible price to our distributors and literally begged them to buy so we could make our junk bond interest payment. But all we heard was, we can't sell it. They were reluctant to invest in our machines because we were a marginal player in the marketplace and had a questionable future. The biggest problem was that our cost reductions were not fully benefiting customers because the supply channel did not adjust their margins to really get the market's attention.

What we did next was unheard of in the industry. We decided to sell new machines at global unreserved public auction. Rithcie Bros. Auctioneers run a very simple but effective method of converting equipment into cash. Their auctions are unreserved. There are no minimum prices. Everything sells to the highest bidder – always. The only thing that one can hope for if selling something is that there is more than one person that wants the product.

Our dealers said Filipov was crazy and that he would kill the business. His response was, "The business is dead – I'm only trying to bring it back to life." The machines did sell, but at 20 percent less than our manufacturing cost. After several auctions with the same results we knew what had to be done. The customer dictated what the price would be for the machines and it was up to Filipov and Waverly to reduce the cost to make a profit. The cost reduction needed to be in excess of 40 percent to make money. The auction company became our second biggest customer that year.

The auctions had another more immediate effect. They moved machines from inventory to the sorely needed cash essential to our survival. As disturbing as it was to industry traditionalists, to use the auction route to sell new machines, it was the breakthrough we needed to move sales forward. It also was a clear signal from Filipov that long standing ways of marketing construction equipment were going to be challenged.

Leon Deutsch continues:

By this time the product lines had been rationalized at the top level. With cost reduction as the number one goal, the next level of product rationalization took place. Each machine was studied piece by piece to reduce cost. Nothing was impossible to the man who came from Bulgaria with nothing.

Leon Deutsch, Craig Lichty and Fil Filipov; The refugee and two farmers from Iowa.

FIL FILIPOV: FILOSOPHIES

Another drastic step was to determine exactly what was available and on order with our suppliers. All open purchase orders with suppliers were cancelled and would be rescheduled only after a complete physical inventory was taken in the plant during November. This had not been done for seven years.

Immediately following this notification to suppliers, the work force was reduced by more than 50 percent. All the remaining people concentrated on building the few orders we had and getting ready for a wall-to-wall inventory.

This action was taken for survival. During the next three months, prior to inventory, engineers were recalled to work on the shop floor and make product improvements and cost reductions. They were not allowed to be in the office during the day, only after hours. People learned how to work smarter, harder and longer in order to survive. We did not lose good people. Everyone knew this was the last chance for the Waverly facility and they had to do everything humanly possible to turn the plant around.

Jerry Stirling, Chairman of the UAW Shop Committee at Koehring Cranes & Excavators, when Fil Filipov came to Waverly, Iowa USA

Fil came to our plant with a lot of different ideas. I didn't agree with a lot of them, but our plant was in bad shape financially with a lot of inventory from Northwest, Mark Industries and our own. With Fil's changes and the hard work from our employees, we turned the plant around to show a profit. One thing about it, Fil did wake up the lifting industry – they know that Terex Lifting is here to stay.

Fil and personal relationships do not mix. There are three ways of doing things: the right way, the union way and Fil's way. But he has gotten it done so far. Now, we will see what the future brings us.

During the period prior to inventory everyone was involved in getting ready to make it the best inventory possible.

A NEW BEGINNING – WAVERLY, IOWA

Inventory was taken in late November and reconciled within one week's time. People worked like they had never worked before. Everyone pulled together and many worked from early morning until late evening. When people saw that Filipov was right there with them during this difficult time something seemed to happen. Even when you didn't expect him, he would show up in his golf cart. I guess they never had golf carts in Bulgaria, so he loved to use one here. Now there were more with Filipov than against him. This was the turning point for the plant.

New orders started to come in as a result of extensive price reductions and improved quality with better delivery schedules. People were starting to be recalled on an as-needed basis. Suppliers started to receive requests to ship components that had been put on hold. Confidence was building. The trend of losing in excess of $1 million per month had changed to making a little money and generating cash. The Bitching, Preaching and Teaching that Filipov practiced was starting to pay off.

The new year seemed like it would never come. Production schedules by model by month were set and adjusted accordingly to customer demands. The extensive hard work had paid off. There was still considerable work to do and modifications to be made. The outsourcing of weldments and machining had reduced lead time considerably. Inventory had been reduced and products had been rationalized. Production levels doubled with less than 50 percent of the people.

Instead of advertising in magazines and trade journals, airline tickets were sent to customers for plant visits. Customer input was solicited for product improvements and new product designs. This had not been done under previous management. The outside world could now see that Waverly had changed. The question now was would it last. Well, last it has. The cranes produced in Waverly now have the highest market share in North America in their class. Yes, there are ups and downs but no one

TEREX LIFTING
Market Share
Hydraulic Rough Terrain and Truck Cranes

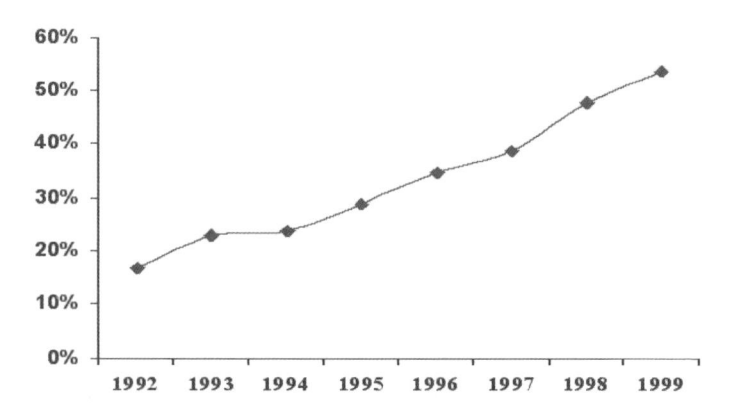

is letting the downs get them down. Filipov is the godfather of this plant and everyone knows it.

In the beginning, Filipov told the people you don't have to like me but you will. Now after seven years under his leadership, there may still be a few people who disagree, but that will always be the case. He would remind us that there is no small village without a cemetery. It has been an interesting ride which is far from over. Who knows what tomorrow will bring for the people in Waverly, Iowa.

Craig Lichty adds:

Through Fil Filipov's leadership and his simple, available and cost effective manufacturing strategy, we were not only able to raise the expectations of something that was less than the industry average but have become a leader that others have tried to imitate.

A NEW BEGINNING – WAVERLY, IOWA

An outsider's perspective. Reprinted with permission from THE CRANE REPORT.

The last time TCR visited Waverly was in February 1993 when Koehring was still being run by previous management. Frankly, the plant – disorganized, congested and untidy – did not make a good impression. The transfer of the Marklift line of aerial work platforms from Brea, California, to Waverly in the late summer of 1992 had clearly not gone well; as is so often the case, the magnitude of the job of relocation seemed to have been seriously underestimated. What's more, the plant already had too much product variety with the ill-conceived 1990 addition of the Northwest line of old mechanical shovels and the 1989 transfer of the Bucyrus-Erie Dynahoe tractor loader backhoes, the most glaring misjudgments. Compounding this situation, last year's addition of the more than 20 different models of Marklift boom and scissor lifts virtually choked the Waverly plant to death. Deliveries, costs and quality all suffered.

Since taking over as CEO in March, Fil Filipov has quite literally transformed Koehring. The manufacturing plant and offices have been dramatically reorganized. The outside areas which were previously stacked high with obsolete and rusting inventory have been cleared and cleaned up. Indeed, inventory levels throughout the operation have been dramatically reduced. Inside the plant there are now clear logically defined production lines, tidy work areas, and good material flow. Operating costs have been reduced by 34 percent so far this year with most of that coming through staff reductions, product improvements, better purchasing, higher productivity and reduced spending.

At a time when Koehring's competitors are making layoffs, all of the shop floor workers who had been laid off last year and earlier this year have been recalled, and the plant is running three shifts. The ranks of salaried employees have been thinned down and, in line with Filipov's principles, everyone is working longer and harder. Lines of communication have been shortened, reducing management tiers from six to three (including Filipov). A renewed sprit among the employees can be seen and felt everywhere. This higher worker morale is showing through in fewer defects and better productivity.

Meeting Fil Filipov for the first time one is struck by his intensity and passion. Clearly this is a man with a mission. He is as likely as not to encapsulate his management philosophy towards a turnaround situation like that at Koehring in the form of a parable. "There's an old story I know about a goldfish," he says. "If you put a fire under the bowl and boil the water, the goldfish will sit there and die. But if you tap the bowl, the fish will jump and escape. I tap on the bowl and make others jump."

He is unequivocal when it comes to the demands he places on his workers. But he at least believes he should set an example. "My basic philosophy in a business turnaround situation is to insist upon everyone working harder, longer and more intelligently. I believe in leading by example, and expect my managers to do the same." Indeed, Filipov himself is no stranger to 18-hour days, often working weekends and holidays. "I try to be everywhere," he says, "checking inventory, looking for cost savings, listening to customers, making sure the machines ship, and managing cash."

Initial reaction from company employees was that he would simply be unable to maintain this pace. "At first everyone round here thought I might last a week or two, then a month, but pretty soon they realized I just wouldn't give up," Filipov recounts. "There are a lot of good people here and it didn't take long for most of them to get on board my train. Those who didn't, notably some middle management, were cut."

What attracted him to the challenge of turning Koehring around, one which involved moving from France to deepest Iowa? "Firstly," he said, "it's the right size. I can get my hands around it. Secondly, I like the Terex management philosophy. They lack the normal corporate bureaucracy and operate a hands-off style – and they're lean and mean. Lastly, and fundamentally, the people here are willing to change and respond to challenges."

And how does he rate his progress to date? "Well I'm not satisfied. I'm never satisfied," he says. Not that progress has not been made, much of which he believes will become apparent in the months and years ahead. "But we're not where I want us to be," Filipov adds, "although we are on the right road, it takes time for many of the changes we've made to flow through to the bottom line. It's very frustrating but we're getting there." Filipov believes the company is becoming faster on its feet and more flexible in its thinking. "We're responding to customers with greater urgency and a `can-do' attitude," he says. "Naturally, after so much disruption, not all of our distributors are as committed to us as I'd like. But that will come. The majority of dealers recognize what we're trying to do here and are very supportive."

Fil Filipov
In March 1994, it was apparent we were on the right track. Leon Deutsch, Craig Lichty and I thought enough of the potential that we put together a business plan in nine days to buy the company. But with Koehring now profitable, Terex Corporation turned down our offer and the operation became the cornerstone and business model for what is now Terex Lifting, the most diversified lifting company in the world with profitable sales of over $1 billion. It is obvious that Terex management made the right decision at the time to keep Koehring as part of the organization.

FIL FILIPOV: FILOSOPHIES

WHAT OTHERS SAY...

Diane Behnke
Terex Cranes
Waverly, Iowa USA
I met Fil Filipov in early 1993 when he came to Terex Waverly as a consultant. Little did I know I would be working for him for the next three years.

We have all heard the saying that something or someone is "one of a kind." Well, that is Fil. He is probably the smartest, most interesting, wildly energetic and unique person I have ever met and had the privilege to work with. On the personal side, he is a very warm, considerate and understanding man with a big heart.

When Fil first came to the Waverly factory and started the turnaround process he is famous for, a lot of employees couldn't believe some of his manufacturing ideas and changes he made that, at the time, seemed so drastic. They doubted him because we had been through so many changes in the past years with little results. Then things started to fall into place and people began to say, "Oh, that's why he did that – it worked." They began to believe in him and respected his decisions.

Howard Lyndon
Terex Lifting
Conway, South Carolina USA
I've worked with Filipov since he first arrived at Koehring Cranes in 1993. It has been a very educational and exciting seven years. In the early years it was sometimes difficult to fully subscribe to the new "Filosophies." But as the results began to show it made the hard work and long hours worthwhile. Fil and his "Filosophies" saved Koehring Cranes, and made Terex Cranes what it is today, the most diversified and successful lifting equipment company in the world, and has completely changed the way business is conducted in our industry. Terex

A NEW BEGINNING – WAVERLY, IOWA

Cranes' business model better positions it to address the new opportunities and challenges as the electronic commerce age engulfs us all.

Dave Stevenson
Terex Cranes
Waverly, Iowa USA
Fil Filipov excels at taking companies on the brink of disaster and restructuring them into profitable operations. What probably impresses me the most is that he does this by using the abilities of the individuals at each location. Fil truly believes that the talents and skills required are best found at each operation rather than bringing in "experts" from the outside. Not only is he quick to evaluate manufacturing opportunities, he is also a master of quickly identifying the individuals that will contribute to the success of an operation. He then entrusts and encourages those employees to take on the challenge of never being satisfied with the status quo. I am not only talking about employees at the supervisor or higher level positions; it has been proven that much of his support comes from the shop floor. I am sure that Fil will always be remembered for his manufacturing excellence, but we should never forget that he is a true leader of people.

Cindy and Larry Trotter
Former owners of Ross Equipment/now United Rental Aerials Cleveland
Cleveland, Ohio
When my husband, Larry, and I first met Fil eight years ago, it was at a critical moment in our business lives. I was owner of Ross Equipment, a distributor of aerial lift equipment. Larry also worked at Ross. For quite some time, our company had been experiencing a variety of problems with one of our major suppliers. It was time to sever the relationship and search for a new partner.

We were contacted by Terex and sent a pair of plane tickets to meet with one Fil Filipov in Waverly, Iowa. We were immediately struck by his enthusiasm, confidence and conviction to lower the price of the product through improved simplicity and efficiency. Our initial thought was his ideas seemed impossible, but the more he talked and the more we saw how his operation reflected his diligence and integrity, the more we believed in him.

For example, while touring the plant, I lost an expensive diamond bracelet. An employee found the bracelet, and it was returned to us before we even made the trip back home. Honest employees were all around him!

"Go not where the path may lead but rather create a path and leave a trail." That's Fil. His business principles, rooted in common sense, have revolutionized our industry and have helped Terex become the force it is today. We followed Fil's trail and expanded our business fivefold. We achieved it by buying at a price that allowed a higher return on investment, while passing the savings on to our customers. The equipment Terex provided was simple and dependable, which lowered our service costs. This is the stuff Fil loves to see happen. Although we have since sold our company, we will always be grateful for Fil's contributions to our success.

Larry and I are most thankful for the friendship we have with Fil and Veronique. Their passion for life and his vibrant personality and tutelage have enriched our lives.

TEREX LIFTING ADVERTISEMENT

WE CONTINUE TO BE COMPETITIVE !

FIL FILIPOV: FILOSOPHIES

V
SIMPLE, AVAILABLE AND COST EFFECTIVE (AND OTHER FILOSOPHIES)

"Simple, Available and Cost Effective – the benchmark to growth"

Passing the savings on to the buyer is the best way for a manufacturer to grow. During my 30 years in the machinery manufacturing industry, I have watched products grow more expensive and complex. Yes, they have also improved in performance, but often, in my opinion, this has been driven by competition between manufacturers rather than by the needs of the user or job.

While improved performance from a machine is almost always welcomed by a customer, the attendant increases in price, maintenance cost and downtime that comes with complexity create excess cost for the user.

If you look at industries like the computer business, every year prices keep coming down while product quality and performance continue to improve. If the computer business can do this, why can't the crane business?

You hear people talk about fixed costs, material costs, labor costs and inflation as excuses for increasing the price of cranes and machinery. But customers are smarter than manufacturers think. They can see the vast sales staffs, layers of management, million dollar trade show exhibits held around the world. They know that it all gets added onto the price of every crane, aerial lift and spare part they purchase.

Twenty years ago, most users purchased their own equipment. Today they most likely lease or rent it. Though rental rates rise and fall according to levels of utilization, over the long term they have progressively declined. Since crane costs have doubled during the past 15 years, it's not surprising that new crane sales are now running at a fraction of their 1970s pace.

Crane buyers are like everyone else. They're looking for the best return on their investment. As a manufacturer, it is in our long-term interest to increase profitability of our buyers. If they make money, they'll grow their businesses and buy more new cranes. If not, they will run their old equipment into the ground or sell out.

Since we cannot directly influence rental rates, our main contribution to the health and wealth of our customers is the cost and earning potential of the equipment we make. Being an operations guy, my main focus has always been to make the product for less money, in less time – not by cutting quality or specification, but by cutting costs and increasing efficiency. During these past four years at Terex, we've succeeded in cutting overhead by 60 percent, increasing productivity by 35 percent and reducing inventory by 40 percent. This has allowed us to reduce our total costs by 15 percent, permitting us to pass on our savings to the customer.

Some people say we're crazy for selling our machines at such low prices and that we could sell just as many if they were just 5-10 percent below the competition. That may or may not be true in the short term. But in the long run, I believe our strategy is the right one.

People make repeat purchases only if they receive a good return on what they buy. The health of the buyer ultimately is equal to the health of the seller. People that rent cranes don't often have huge facilities, massive marketing teams, corporate

SIMPLE, AVAILABLE AND COST EFFECTIVE

jets, fleets of fancy cars. Why should we?

(The above was reprinted with permission from Lift Equipment Magazine)

The dramatic progress made under my leadership in the last few years is the perfect example of the validity of *Simple, Available and Cost Effective*.

Virtually every step taken was to position our machines and organization as simple both to use and maintain, readily available, and an exceptional value delivering good return on investments.

Everything we did was based on the objective of making two plus two equal at least five. Too many times I have observed consolidations made for the sake of consolidating. Consolidations could lead to bureaucracy – bureaucracy that will not be good for business. I make every effort to keep things simple in both organizations and products.

Simplicity does not mean basic, but meeting the customer's needs. By minimizing electronic and other unnecessary bells and whistles and concentrating on fewer models with competitive specifications and capabilities we provide a user friendlier alternative, one that is easier to service for greater dependability. Emphasis is on simplifying the product until it's so tight, that not a single part on the unit is superfluous. We listen to what users want and quickly react to their needs. We make sure that the product is always available when the customer needs it – including beating the competitor's prices by as much as 20 percent.

We have not increased prices in eight years. Not increasing prices does several things; makes you find ways to reduce cost, refuse price increases from suppliers, increase productivity, and puts enormous pressure on the competition. None of this makes good sense if the customer cannot benefit from it.

Availability is also a direct result of how we go to market. It is my belief that the most effective way to create value to the customer – and create a competitive environment – is to avoid exclusivity and territories. Let whoever can add value to the product sell the product. Not only will it create more market exposure, it will stabilize product prices around a more realistic figure. A dealer who knows he is the only one selling the product has no competition and can charge whatever he wants. A reseller who must compete with others in the same area must keep prices reasonable and provide excellent product support, which leads to more sales and wider market coverage. All of this translates into a better market share keeping everyone in the chain honest and the customer happy.

However, as we often hear, every rule has an exception and this also holds true here. If we have a distributor or user who has a huge market share in their area or can guarantee predetermined volumes, I am happy to work with such aggressive organizations and bend the rules. Results are all that count.

Step number one in this process is to abandon the idea that a distributor is the customer. He is effectively a local agent who provides service and product support. This is valuable and important. Well run distributors can be very profitable, but greed can take over which often leads to a loss of market share. If a distributor attempts to make too great a margin relative to the services provided, he can become vulnerable to the e-technology if more aggressive, lower cost alternatives are made available.

Think of him as a business partner, think of him as a profit center, think of him as an extension of corporate structure, but never ever think of him as the customer. His one and only relationship with us is defined by how well he sells and services our product for both parties to make reasonable profits.

Some distributors are running important rental fleets and that part of their activity is considered as the customer. Leasing and renting of equipment will continue to increase and provide respectable returns on the invested capital.

SIMPLE, AVAILABLE AND COST EFFECTIVE

This type of thinking does not make many people happy – suppliers with no price increases, manufacturers with thinner margins, distributors with a very competitive environment and lower margins – this all puts pressure on sales people, and big pressure on the competition. The CUSTOMER is the only winner and only the disciplined will survive.

By the same token, if performance is expected from the sales and distribution network, it must be pampered with rapid, frequent, first-priority contact. Always be available with a short notice, call or fax, and make sure the seller can get to us if we are needed. We must be there to provide technical information and support at all times.

With the right product and product support, the right price and proper financing I often say, "We do not sell – we take orders." In most cases, I don't like to spend a lot of time developing our own sales force. At times, it just doesn't make sense, and if we look closely at sales people, we will see why. About half the time, they are not happy because they are not paid as much as the competition, take credit during good economies and blame pricing, product performance or product quality during tough times. What are they typically trying to sell – an overpriced product? They have to travel all the time to see customers, so they have to have a car, but yet they're normally traveling by plane, so who is using the car? The customer ends up paying the bill!

In my opinion and Filosophy there are better ways to make contact with the customers. Rather than trying to go into the marketplace and find customers hoping to convince them with sales gimmicks drummed up by some marketing whiz, why not try something simple, if old-fashioned? Bring the customers to the manufacturing site and let them look over the products as they come together.

I am sure that the world will continue to evolve, but for

now I have found that one of the most effective ways is an open house. Clean the place up, organize leisurely factory tours, have new products available for demonstration and user input. It is also a good time to open the facilities to employees and their families, making them proud of the place they spend most of their time in. Have a nice barbecue!

Rather than spending thousands of dollars for salespeople to carry glossy brochures and charge for expensive entertainment, give the lavish treatment to the customers. Why not let the customer use the equipment for a limited time and convince him that this is the machine that will make him money.

Be flexible and act instead of react. In the last few years we have acquired several well known brand names putting them under one umbrella. In the course of absorbing these acquisitions, our attention was taken away from product support which our competition was quick to try to capitalize on. We quickly responded by creating a special support program. Customer service representatives with special vans are strategically located to respond quickly and enhance the support capabilities of the distribution organization. Problem identified, effective response delivered. The lesson: Competition will take you down given the chance, will spy on you, only if they fear you will get their business. They will also respect you if you get it done.

A PLACE FOR EVERYTHING

Keep the supplier base small. Many companies have teams that do nothing but build up frequent flier miles, checking out and certifying suppliers. It's important to do the quality assurance, but a team of 4-6 people is way too much. I believe that only one or two people should travel. As for how many suppliers? Well, 52 is not too many – I can call one every week, can visit one every month and can more readily keep up.

SIMPLE, AVAILABLE AND COST EFFECTIVE

At any rate, once we have material, we have to keep track of it. Like it or not, good housekeeping is essential for good work. Scattering things is natural – the universe works that way. Cleaning things up is custodial work, and it's menial, but preventing messes from occurring is called management. Not enough people give enough credit these days to the adage, *"A place for everything, and everything in its place."* As soon as there is disorder, the cost goes up. There's also a bigger aspect of disorder. Think about it: How do we feel when the house is clean, as opposed to unkempt? When our surroundings are clean and in place, we feel more comfortable. Disorder and a lack of organization weigh on our spirits and distract us from doing our best. How many people would want to sit in someone's filthy kitchen and have a chat? Not many. If we don't do something about it, though, we become acclimated to it. This is a dangerous situation to be in, especially from a quality point of view. A clean place produces quality products at lower cost.

A major part of every acquisition's *100 Days Pain for Gain* action plan has to do with some form of housekeeping. Obsolete and unused materials are disposed of and the balance placed in an orderly and strategic manner. Supplier relationships are reviewed and usually reduced; outsourcing options are pursued where savings can be affected. It is not unusual to enlist the services of all employees – including management on a Saturday – to address a problem and make the necessary progress. And the focus on housekeeping and inventory reduction is not a one-time event. Every plant and office has the poster on the following page prominently displayed:

TEREX LIFTING

a Place for Everything & Everything in its Place

GOOD HOUSEKEEPING
=
QUALITY & COST EFFECTIVE PRODUCTS

SIMPLE, AVAILABLE AND COST EFFECTIVE

KEEP IT SIMPLE

I have often found that things that are too complex, indirect or hard to follow, are really hiding a weak spot. Maybe the person who designed the machine didn't think it through very well, or maybe there are potential legal problems that nobody wants to touch. That's because, when we think about it, nearly every problem we run into can be handled with straightforward common sense – if we think about it. The more convoluted arguments become, the greater the chances that someone is holding onto an outdated idea, probably for sentimental reasons. People can say what they will, but I think most businesses can be run a lot simpler.

As an example of simplicity, consider products. Finished machines ought to be for sale, but so many people don't bother to ask the kind of questions that need to be asked. True, sometimes it's painful to think about why products aren't selling, and it's nearly impossible for most people to answer those kinds of questions objectively. Who's going to demo them? Why aren't they selling? Are our competitors selling? Is it product design, cost, market, something we're missing or not participating in? Is our stuff obsolete with no security for the future?

An example was the redesign of the control panels on our articulating boom aerial work platforms. Basically, it is the same control panel, but now has a simple function display that lets the operator know which way the machine will move before he touches the switch. Before, he needed to think which part of the machine was going to move before touching a switch. Sometime ago the watch industry introduced the digital watch. How many do you see around now? Not many. Why? I think because we do not want to read what time it is, we want to see what time it is. We normally only look at the location of the watch hands and determine the time.

Looking closely at machines in a manufacturing facility, we can, I'm sure, see some machines that just aren't efficient – an investment may be necessary, or we might just need to eliminate tools and equipment that no one is using. I'll spare you all the gory details, you can figure them out on your own: Things like reducing maintenance and repair time, consolidating some machines, eliminating older for newer more flexible machines and so on. If the volume is there and we take the time to assess these assets, opportunities for improvement can be found.

Why would anyone lease a fax? Why would anyone lease a car? If someone has a company car, they justify the lease because they want to choose the car themselves and change it more often because they are going to use it for their own good. How many CEOs wanting to change the location of their headquarters, end up locating them close to their own homes?

Looking for a contrast to *Simple, Available and Cost Effective*? Look no farther then the computer industry with its constant upgrade philosophy. It's not my Filosophy. In fact, the computer arena is really the flukiest segment around because software is where the money is made. You don't have to be Bill Gates to know that. As long as we have executives and managers who cannot go in and put their hands on the system and understand what they're buying, computer companies will always make loads of money. Manage something you can't understand, and you tend to mystify and deify it beyond belief. In the case of the computer industry, it seems like mysticism, but it's really nothing more than just another set of industry slang. Once we get the hang of it, we discover that computer professionals put their pants on one leg at a time, just like the rest of us, and – trust me on this one – they know how good they have it. They even have their own code of silence to protect it. If you talk to managers of a computer company and ask them why the machines must be upgraded so frequently, you get back a line of zealous marketing and no real answer. If they had to deal with me, their revenues would be one tenth of what they earn today, and the software would be much simpler. Most of the personal computers and notebooks that I see are like the human brain: only used to about 10 percent of capacity and full of errors. You don't need to constantly double processor speed and try to cram the entire encyclopedia of the western world on the hard drive to get some work done.

Even the Internet is hyped beyond belief. Yes, it's nice to have a global computer network, but does anyone remember the hoopla surrounding the international telephone systems? I'm sure if we go back in the library archives and read those newspapers, we will see the same sentiment. Perhaps it will be expressed in dated language, but the excitement and the zeal about "emerging technologies" and the "future of enterprise" will be there in one form or another. That's why concepts like network computers don't get me too worked up. Granted, they are an interesting idea, built around the same model as the telephone, with most of the smarts "somewhere out there" and the home unit acting mainly as a terminal. Still, it looks like just another way to guarantee a large revenue stream. Imagine being told every time you turn the thing on that you need new software because it's been upgraded. Oh, and by the way, we need your credit card number on file so we can keep taking larger and larger payments. This entire "constant upgrade" process is nothing more than a scam. Imagine trying to sell a piece of heavy equipment to a customer, telling them you're going to automatically charge them 15 percent per month for maintenance.

"Oh, sorry, sir, the equipment is going to change, and the fittings probably aren't tight so you're going to have leaks. This 15 percent a month is just to make sure you're happy. Oh, and by the way, this machine will only work right for about six months, then you'll have to upgrade to a new model." We would be out of business in about six hours.

Upgrades are nothing more than a new version of one program that was never developed well enough in the first place. Why pay for a new version every six months or two years, when we can use what we already have? Computer people are successfully selling wind and calling it "research and development."

Why didn't they take the time to look at what the business actually needed to begin with? So what if my spelling isn't corrected on the spot? How many millions are spent on software? How many millions on maintenance? How many on training? How many millions are wasted? Clearly it's a perfect opportunity for a never-ending stream of revenue. In the process, they severely disrupt the business and generally make false statements about productivity improvements. In truth, about 90 percent of the businesses that use computers do not need upgrades all that bad, and so often. You don't need a new system every two years to get efficiency. Simple, available and cost effective – those terms certainly don't apply to the computer industry. Remeber, nothing is forever. It's only a matter of time before people get fed up with the upgrade merry-go-round.

WHAT OTHERS SAY...

Edward Samera
Terex Lifting VP
Cedarburg, Wisconsin USA
Traditionally, people in the lifting industry were ego driven when developing products. If one company made a 40-foot scissor lift, then another was determined to make a 50 footer, and then the race was on to have the tallest aerial lift every year, regardless of what the market would bear. Products were created as a matter of personal accomplishment instead of customer needs, costs and profits. Price was determined

by cost plus 35 percent and higher margins with the price in the marketplace dictated by the manufacturer. High cost, large margin and low manufacturing volumes made it difficult to make money.

This all changed with Fil Filipov and his drive to provide products that are simple to use and maintain, easy to manufacture and particularly cost effective. Focus is on listening to what the customer needs and producing those products that make good business sense.

He goes after the heart of the marketplace, avoiding special purpose machines, eliminating redundant models and discontinuing low-volume, high-cost models. Engineers are challenged to be more creative, shorten design time, use common components wherever possible, lower cost through higher purchasing volume and make servicing and training easier. He also approaches cost reduction with unrelenting intensity, outsourcing where it makes sense and using technologies from other industries.

Low-cost, high-volume machines with moderate margins making greater profit in the long term is Fil's way. His distaste for bureaucracy also is a big assist in getting products to market faster.

Bob Litchev
BGI USA, Inc
Burr Ridge, Illinois USA

Since I met Fil Filipov five years ago at an industry show in Miami, I have always tried to understand what was the thing that makes this man a leader. Maybe it is his obsession for detail or his ability to look behind difficult circumstances for new ideas and opportunities.

His unparalleled positive attitude that enables him to look ahead each and every day with all the eagerness and optimism of the young is an inspiration to all his friends.

These qualities beneath the surface of his tough and demanding exterior make him the leader that many want to follow.

FIL FILIPOV: FILOSOPHIES

VI
QUALITY AND TURNAROUNDS

Many people have written books about quality and I agree with the statement that quality is not a trip, it is a journey – a never ending journey.

No turnaround can be considered a success if the quality is not there. When I talk about quality, I don't just mean product quality. I mean quality in everything we do; how the receptionist answers the phone, how the orders are placed, how accurate are delivery promises and last, but not least, the quality of the information flowing in and out of the company.

Cutting quality during a turnaround is detrimental – no corners should be cut, no expense should be spared. Reducing cost does not mean making it cheap. Make versus buy does not mean no one else can do it better. It is a change, and change is a must during turnarounds.

The story goes, when getting a new job, you find in your empty desk drawer, three envelopes, marked number 1, 2 and 3. Instructions are that when you make your first mistake, close the door of your office and open envelope number one. It says, "Blame your predecessor." When you make the second big mistake, you close the door and open envelope number two. You read again, "Blame your predecessor." When finally you make your third mistake and open the last envelope the message says, "Prepare your three envelopes."

FIL FILIPOV: FILOSOPHIES

If you had to pick a single word to characterize my business success it would be turnarounds. I don't ever remember having to prepare three envelopes. My history is replete with successful examples.

Turnaround is not a dirty word. But, as the old saying goes, you can't malke an omelet without breaking eggs. Unfortunately, it often is associated with the seemingly callous, arbitrary dismissal of employees for the benefit of the stockholders. It can also be the difference between an ongoing viable business or closed doors with even greater worker disruption.

I grow businesses, not close them. For a variety of reasons including the quantum changes being brought about by the global marketplace, the management and investors in old-line companies faced a decision time for their future and some opted to leave the construction equipment business. Terex Corporation saw these situations as opportunities and seized them knowing that its strategy of cost reduction combined with product and component synergies could build sales, market share and, most importantly, profits.

Having established a track record in this area, I was given the opportunity by Terex to create, from practically nothing, what has become the most diversified lifting company in the world. To me it was a natural progression from my personal work ethic to establishing the regime of hard, focused effort necessary to turn a decaying situation into something viable and ongoing.

We have been able to change well-known but dying franchises into ongoing, profitable businesses. During numerous acquisitions over the past six years, we have been able to revive and integrate such equipment brands as Northwest, BCP, Koehring, Lorain, Marklift, PPM, P&H, Bendini, Brimont, Simon, RO, Telelect, Cella, BPI, Holland Lift, American, Italmacchine, Peiner, Comedil, Matbro, Moffett, Princeton, Kooi Aap, and Franna.

QUALITY AND TURNAROUNDS

Before I give you some examples, let me explain my approach.

I come in and work like a surgeon: Cut once, cut deep and get the job done. It's like a cancerous tumor, if it is not removed entirely, the cancer will remain and spread. From my perspective, I have to act decisively and immediately, so not to leave the sword hanging over everyone's head. Especially when things aren't going well, I can't constantly re-open the wound if the patient is to recover. Otherwise, the risk is creating a serious morale problem. For whatever reason, this takes about nine months to carry through. I have always said that if a baby can be born in nine months, then a business can be re-born in that same period. There's no good reason why it works out that way, but it does. It also works out to be a four-stage process, as I have confirmed during numerous turnaround efforts. I significantly reduce staff, other employees leave voluntarily, I adjust, and finally make some new hires.

I start by cutting high-level and middle management positions which I believe are irrelevant to the success of the company. This is when some people call me a dictator – I like to think of myself as a benevolent dictator. The cut is deep and immediate, usually within a few days of my arrival. Essentially, I'm deciding who gets on the boat with me. That's not to say that it's a slash and burn approach – I choose based on loyalty, effort and personal concern for the business. Commitment shows, and I reward it, even when things are not looking so good.

Let me assure you that I do have sleepless nights and it is not as easy as it might sound. Like in any profession, there has to be a degree of know-how experience, priority plus simply, some gut feel. For a turnaround person, there is no in between. Many have tried and failed because there is no formula, it is different every time.

In most cases I am helped by an anonymous letter, a phone

call, or am stopped in the shop by people who care, who give me some idea where to look. My relentless drive to fix the business is soon unerstood and people try to help. As always, a high degree of judgment is required.

This is a good place to talk about how to downsize. I advocate a humane – some may say socialist – approach. I don't believe in just throwing good people out. It's bad for them, it's bad for me and it's bad for the business. Separating is tragic, whether in your career or your personal life. Downsizing and restructuring quickly improves a company's results, so there's no reason to be stingy with separation pay. In my opinion, layoffs should not be something that you wait to justify by the state of the economy or "current conditions in the industry." In today's environment, these kinds of adjustments are necessary nearly all the time. I have never participated in the popular theory of reducing people's salaries. I have never seen this work.

Continuous improvement is not as easy as it looks, but it is absolutely the only way to succeed. These constant adjustments are like engineering changes, such as the improvements that have been made to the 911 Porsche through the years. The Porsche remains one of the best built cars even though it was designed nearly half a century ago. Viewed from the outside, there are really not that many differences from the first one to the most recent model. Underneath, however, and worked into the design are millions of small adjustments, continuous changes that amount to doing things a little bit better every year. That's why it is the car that it is today, and it provides a model that companies will probably have to adopt in order to compete.

Issues and problems must constantly be addressed making whatever adjustments are necessary to keep the business "tuned

FOLLOW THE THREE RS: RESPECT FOR SELF. RESPECT FOR OTHERS. RESPONSIBILITY FOR ALL YOUR ACTIONS

QUALITY AND TURNAROUNDS

up." These days, not only is it true that nothing is forever, but things hardly stay the same from quarter to quarter. Often an entire business area will turn completely around overnight, and not making the necessary changes to accommodate these ups and downs can lead to big trouble.

On the other hand, making adjustments when there is good reason for the adjustments, employee morale will suffer to a lesser degree than if several major restructurings are undertaken. Employees will often look at what has been done and recognize that they would do the same thing in your shoes.

There is no question that companies across the globe will continue to adjust by downsizing as productivity goes up. As a result, it is imperative that top management find better, less disruptive ways to handle layoffs. One suggestion I have is making it easier, and more financially attractive, for those employees who are already thinking about leaving.

There are some people who are not happy with their job, or who know that they are not or cannot contribute much to the company, but are afraid of taking that first step. If they are encouraged with a reasonable severance package, some will take that step and ease the apprehension of those who want to stay. I fail to understand why some companies have no problem giving golden parachutes to high-level executives, yet search for cheapest way possible at the lower levels. Cheap doesn't mean efficient, and it certainly doesn't help an already difficult situation.

Others dream about starting their own businesses – in some cases, businesses that could complement the company. Why not offer a good severance package so he or she can go ahead and start their own shop? Let them find out what it is like to run a business, to make money, and to see if they will put in the same working hours. Before you know it, that little business might be so well-established that it can take the place of a department, reducing your overhead. The rules need to be changed so that people don't have to get fired to get a severance. Otherwise, the ticking of the "downsizing time bomb" contributes to serious decreases in productivity.

At any rate, when I first approach a bloated organization, I try to measure twice and cut once. The major criteria for these cuts are the organizational structure, including the number of levels, the pay-to-performance ratio and total expense. I look long and hard at expenses to find whether someone runs the business as if it were his or her own – these are perhaps the strongest indicators of someone's commitment to the business. Surprisingly, I have discovered people charging monthly alimony to expense accounts. I've found salesmen sitting around in hotel rooms watching pornographic movies, and executives spending two or three weeks "checking out" the site of a potential trade show or conference in advance.

Two things must be critically important to the employee: the business, and their family. People who expect their employer to shell out big bucks for entertainment will be disappointed if they work for me. To put it another way, they aren't going to be working for me. It's the sense that the person is dedicated both to the business and to his or her family: If you're going to be away from home on business, you should get done what you need to get done and get home. It's what you owe your family, and it's what you owe your company. I expect nothing less from myself.

That's also one of the reasons that honest effort plays such a big role in who goes and who stays. If people aren't pulling their weight, we just have no room for them in business. When you're at work, you should be working – I expect at least that much dedication. I expect my top people to come in on Saturday and at least do some thinking on Sunday, so the rest of the employees will have a job. When I consistently don't get good performance from a particular employee, I have to figure that person is in the wrong line of work. If we don't love what we are doing, if it doesn't excite us enough to make us want to work hard, we probably should be doing something else. I jump out of bed every morning, knowing that I've got a full agenda of things I love doing. I know down to the item what I'm going to do when I arrive at work in the morning. If you don't have the same kind of attitude, then something's wrong and you need to find out how to fix it. You may not be in the best situation – we all have ups and downs – but at least you can be excited about the giant steps you're going to take to get out of the situation. Anything less is painful, counter-productive and just plain crazy.

Once the clean quick, first cut is done and I have eliminated the largest percentage of dispassionate employees, I wait for the next mode, which comes about 4-6 weeks later. This is the inevitable exodus that follows the appropriate reductions. These are people who were incensed by the first cuts, who had friends in the first group, or who just flat don't want to work for me. It's tough to lose good workers in this "fallout cut," but I'd much rather have people on the job who feel motivated to help turn the business around than those who are focused on other, not-so-relevant criteria.

And, of course, there's a third mode – performance. Whatever I have left after my first few adjustments, which often include promotions for people who are performing, there are still some who are not living up to expectations, or who can't handle the changes necessary to turn the business around. The changes already implemented require drastic changes in working habits, and to be quite honest, some people find this very difficult to accept.

Finally, after all this is done, about nine months down the road, you hire just a few people in jobs you simply cannot fill from within. I do try to promote from within because almost invariably we find what we need. By that point, the pain caused by the reductions has subsided, because people have had the chance for promotions and more money. Employees accept people brought in from the outside because they know the new folks were hired to do things that the existing work force couldn't – or wouldn't – do. They've also come to the realization that half the workforce really can produce twice the profits. It seems that no matter where I go, I can always double productivity by eliminating non-productive people.

In 1987, after my employer had been bought twice, the latest parent company purchased a well-known French manufacturer. Based on my previous performance, probably my knowledge of the French industry, and the necessity of a major restructuring, I was put in charge. As I love to say, no matter where you go, you always find the same problems. Even though their product turned over hundreds of millions per year, using five plants and enjoying a 50 percent market share, I looked at the overhead and saw there was a lot of fat built up around the belt.

Upper management asked me to sit on the Board of Directors and serve as general manager of the acquired company. I couldn't have asked for a better briar patch. For just the second time on a massive scale, I applied my "Filosophies," simplifying operations, reducing bureaucracy and eliminating non-value-added management.

It was at this point that a lot of industry segments began to refer to me as the "cost cutter." Someone even called me "the man who sounds like Churchill, but is not" – probably because I constantly stressed working harder, longer and smarter to accomplish the chosen objectives. I do not think I can stress this enough. You can spend hundreds of thousands of dollars on management seminars, training classes, consulting help and the best business books; you can hire dozens of people with the right degrees from prestigious institutions and give them key positions; you can do everything that common sense and conventional wisdom tell you are the right things; but if you do not work longer hours, put more effort into your work and make smarter decisions than your competition, you simply will not succeed, period. Your objectives must be the most important thing, and until you understand this fact and act on it, you will have a tough time creating a great company.

Once I practice these principles, however, I find that overhead and non-value-added labor really begins to grate. These kinds of overhead problems spelled the beginning of the end for me at my first career company. It came in the early 1990s, during a major slowdown of the industry. It wasn't the slowdown that sent me on my way, however, but disgust with a glutted management culture that needed drastic reductions to get out of profit's way. In 1988, I was promoted as one of the company's first vice presidents in Europe. Within the next 14 months, the number of vice presidents grew to 43. The new president had done a great job in the original restructuring, turning the company into a lean and mean operation making profits. But soon after he repeated the mistakes so often made by others, adding way too much overhead. And he got caught.

Knowing him personally, I paid him a visit and in a polite way told him that he was becoming like the Shah of Iran. I explained to him that I did not like the bureaucracy he was creating and that things were not going that well in the operations; that there was too much bureaucracy and too many people doing things that had nothing to do with the bottom line. Administrative costs were skyrocketing, and at times far too many people were on airplanes. For some of them, going to Europe had become an ongoing holiday on the company.

Basically, there were far too many chiefs for the number of productive indians. Much of the action on executive row involved 10 or 12 cousins all debating non-issues. In a word, I was jaded and ready to get out. When I told him I no longer enjoyed my work and wanted to get out, he said, "If you dance with the bear, it's the bear that decides when to let go, not you." Before he could even try to help me get out, events happened and he was gone. The bear was now gone and I was dancing alone.

I left the company in 1992, and I'm glad I did. The company simply didn't understand one of the key factors in any business, of any size: simplicity in running the operation – even if profitable with a stable product and a respectable share. We all know the rest of the story. Nothing is forever!

Within months after departing Case Tenneco, I had several offers on the table. One of them involved a major manufacturer in Europe, a $350 million business with 24 plants. I studied it carefully and found the organization didn't look all that different from the one I had just left – dozens of levels hiding advanced bureaucracy, just the kind of place to go in and shake up. But I was certain this would not be allowed.

Ron DeFeo had already joined Terex Corporation when he called me about Koehring Cranes & Excavators, in Waverly, Iowa. What happened next, as you have read, is the subject of an entire chapter in this book.

In 1994, I was given the additional responsibility of restructuring the European division of Clark Material Handling Company, a forklift producer that belonged to Terex at the time. Same problems, same issues, different country.

When I arrived in Germany, it was a $100 million business losing money. Entire branches seemed to be doing very little – not just riding out a low period, but producing absolutely nothing. The product was far too complicated and not cost effective, and the product lines were not relevant to the markets. I got right to work and results soon followed. Staff was drastically reduced, all but two of the 36 big and expensive company cars were eliminated, administrative buildings were closed and offices were moved into the plant. I have always felt that managers need to see exactly what's going on with the product at all times. Some of my favorite pictures show myself and my entire management staff with our offices in the center of the manufacturing facility, where we can "feel" the heartbeat of the factory. As I once told an employee, out there I don't have to see what's going on, I can hear it. The change was dramatic: Production, which lagged at 2,800 units, jumped to more than 4,000 units. Moreover, we sold what we made at a profit in a stable market. We did it by ruthlessly eliminating waste, and by taking market share from our competitors with products that were simpler, more reliable, easier to use and less costly.

Remember, I do not cut productive workers or eliminate profitable projects. In many situations, it's almost as if the garden has been left unattended, allowing the weeds to creep in and choke off the harvest. Without constant care, the weeds of busi-

Managing on the factory floor in Conway, South Carolina during the restructuring of the PPM/P&H factory.

ness – outdated products, wasteful procedures, laziness – tend to spring up quickly. I take swift, decisive action to eliminate anything that doesn't contribute. It may sound harsh, but that kind of quantum improvement in productivity is what's necessary to keep up with worldwide competition.

It was always my wish to continue the restructuring of Clark Material Handling in the United States, but Terex, having taken Clark Material Handling back to profitability, sold it at a $50 million profit to focus its resources on becoming a major player in the crane business.

Which brings me back to Iowa. All in all, it was a very good decision to go there. The work ethic was good and several of the managers I met there continue as major contributors on my staff. Within a year the plant was making a slight profit, and to make a long story short, we eventually improved our position to the point where we could buy out a major player.

The mobile crane businesses we acquired were awash in inefficiency, and I immediately moved in with my famous "100 Days/Pain for Gain" program, a very specific action plan covering every aspect of the business with responsibility assigned to every line. (A general example is included in the appendix.)

I have always achieved the best results by going in and making the most radical changes in the first 100 days, and that certainly worked in this case. We managed to eliminate about 20 percent of useless cost in a very short time by following my 8Ms. This wasn't easy, either, because the acquired company had a massive outlay in facilities around the world. In fact, it was a long, bumpy ride. The business was sicker than anyone expected, so a lot of risks had to be taken, one tiny decision at a time, to get it back on its feet. We succeeded. In the first full year

OPEN YOUR ARMS TO CHANGE, BUT DON'T LET GO OF YOUR VALUES

after the takeover, sales were up, as were profits. Chalk up one more victory for *Simple, Available and Cost Effective*, and it came about because it was just flat working. It's still working today, and I honestly think it will work for just about anyone in any situation.

With the successful restructuring and integration of this acquisition, we now had the critical mass to get the attention of the lifting industry – equipment users, distributors, suppliers, media and the financial community.

Cost Reductions
There is a Chinese proverb that says, "LOW PROFIT – SELL A LOT."

By now you know that I like the volume market, and that making money in a business is not an option for any business. It shouldn't be!

I have only submitted myself to an executive consultant, or should I say an industrial shrink, one time. Here is some of what he said about me 15 years ago:

"Filipov demonstrated an ability to think critically and analytically in many of the positions he held ... He involves himself very, very heavily in his work and to that extent makes use of his ability ... He is a high result-oriented person who willingly works extremely hard for however long is necessary to get the job done ... He has a strong, intense sense of urgency about completing work in a minimum amount of time."

Critical and analytical hard work is what cost reductions are about. Driving cost reductions is probably the thing I am known for, loved and hated for, recognized and respected in the field. Let me confess to you – it is not a part time job either. For so many years I watched people accept price increases, wage increases, productivity and efficiency declines, overhead increasing, and all I would witness in management meetings were excuses and well-structured blames to someone else. When my time came I committed to NO PRICE INCREASES in the products we were selling. People took me for naïve and suicidal. This was eight years ago. Yes, eight consecutive years without an increase – an even better product for less, eight years later.

Why did I do it?

No other choice was available unless we wanted to be led by the competition. We chose to lead, to become the troublemakers and live up to our promises. Before going into cost reduction, let's agree on the basic ingredients of the cost of any product. I don't care what the product is, it has three cost elements:

COST = MATERIAL + LABOR + OVERHEAD

I attack every element of cost but find different solutions for each. The objectives change constantly and the results are astonishing. It is not even polite to try to generalize this very important subject, so I will give you some ideas on how I do it.

First of all, nothing will happen if I do not create the Cost Reduction Religion with constant follow up. Everything must be questioned relentlessly – what was good yesterday is no longer good tomorrow. This is one reason I do not understand and do not approve of supply contracts. I firmly believe that every material, labor and overhead cost can be reduced.

It's like anything else. I started running figuring it was one of the best ways to keep my weight down after I quit smoking 10 years ago. Initially, I was able to run a mile and a half in 30 minutes. A colleague said he could run a mile in less than 10 minutes and I thought he was lying. But as I continued to work at it, I was also able to get under 10 minutes, then two miles under 20 minutes and then three miles in 30 minutes. Men, like French wine, get better with age.

I first establish aggressive objectives. If you do not know – try for half! I know you are already thinking I am crazy. It is fine to think it but I am sure when you try it and when it works, I will gain your respect. I have done it so many times!

Know the numbers, the percentages. How much do you purchase, from where and from whom? What percentage does material represent in your total cost? Unless it is a computer software company where material is not very much, the material is the first opportunity. It is the first thing that I attack with a passion. For me everything is a question of comparison, a question of reasonable and justifiable cost. I do compare costs by weight. If I had it my way, equipment would be sold by the ton.

One of the first places I look for purchasing cost reductions is in the receiving department. I feel guilty if I do not go and visit the place, and I hope every manufacturing person will do the same at their facility after reading this book. Reports are fine as indicators, but the visits allow me to visualize several different aspects of the manufacturing process. First, the receiving area is never close to the offices so it is good exercise. On the way there, I can check on a quality problem, improve the housekeeping in a specific area, contribute to productivity with some ideas, watch for unsafe practices, talk to an employee and then, here I am – in Receiving.

Many times I have discovered that the part in the box is worth less then the shipping cost, or that the computer continues to order something we have stopped using, or that the supplier, while not increasing his prices, has been allowed to charge for extra packaging. There is no way I can or will describe all of the things that can be found there, but I can assure you I find something every time. It is impossible to go to any receiving department and not see opportunities for cost reductions!

I ask others and myself how much should an item cost? How much would I pay if I were buying it with my money and for my own use? How much does it weigh? What is the cost per

ONCE A YEAR, GO SOME PLACE YOU'VE NEVER BEEN BEFORE

pound? How many times are parts moved around before used? If I asked these questions, in most cases people understood and moved ahead on their own. Cost reductions are not one person's responsibility, it is the job of every one in an organization.

One of my first steps in manufacturing rationalization is to identify and eliminate items that the factory cannot add value to. Reduction of the supplier base is often talked about but not often implemented – it is a must. I often try to avoid the lengthy time of quoting parts and instead give target prices. Since these target prices are only temporary, it allows the supplier a chance to get in faster, but also to be able to make it at a profit. None of our suppliers should act as our Red Cross – I realize that and want them to be profitable.

In my mind there are no such things as fixed costs. All costs are variable and subject to revision based on volume.

When I came to Waverly, Iowa, computer lease and maintenance costs were $56,000 per month. Can you believe this? The place was losing one million dollars per month and the computer cost was never even questioned! I call this WIND. It took countless phone calls and threats for repossession of the equipment. When the people started calling us on Saturday afternoon, we knew we had their attention. The open lease was converted to a short low-cost buyout. We had the computer paid off in 18 months for half the price, plus we now had ownership. If necessary, I was prepared to let them take their equipment and run the place with PCs.

If you want it bad enough, you can reduce any cost – nothing is fixed. When I look at how telephone companies are continuing to fight for the business and reducing costs to the user, I am convinced that we can all do it. There is no gain without pain. Engineers are key to a good working cost reduction program. Talented, questioning, provocative engineers have taken people to the moon, but slow, sleepy, stubborn and arrogant engineers also are responsible for the downfall of some famous brands. I am sure we can all name a few.

One of my most frustrating experiences is the misunderstanding that a cost-reduced product is a cheap product. Most of the time the originators are competitors in their effort to slow down the process.

Provocative thinking in any industry is looked at as predatory, but I do think that it is the kind of thinking necessary for progress. Protectionism at times is what holds back the progress. I hope to see us all make strides in the areas of environmentally friendlier products – electric versus hydraulic, electric versus internal combustion. Also, lighter products – plastic versus steel, aluminum versus steel, composites versus steel, radio controlled versus cables, laser versus cable and who knows what other new material tomorrow may bring us.

I owe my openness, I think, to the fact that I do not allow myself to fall in love with any given technology and process. I am proud of my reputation for being a relentless driver of cost reduction in whatever industry I have been in.

WHAT OTHERS SAY...

Mariano and Martina Moritsch
Comedil Tower Cranes
A Unit of Terex Lifting
Fontanafredda, Italy
We met Fil for the first time at Intermat '97 and immediately found his way of running a business, especially his direct and straight approach to people, very similar to ours.

They can call it charisma, but it is not only that. It is not easy in this field, traditionally not very innovative, to find people who firmly believe that they can change well-established rules to make it better not only for the manufacturer but especially for the final end user. Every evolution comes through a revolution. We think Fil has been the head of this revolution.

Some things will go his way, some others may not, but in any case, he gives all actors in this circus something to think about, at least the most important things. From our personal point of view, we prefer to work with people like Fil that demand a lot, but speak straight and listen to all suggestions, and give confidence and responsibility when things work well.

Chris Melia
Longtime Friend
United Kingdom
Right from the start, Fil's approach was the same as now. In the early 1980s, at the start of his first appointment as a plant manager, he set about transforming the operation: tearing down old buildings, relocating assembly and refocusing the business. The initial reaction from his colleagues was amazement that so many changes could happen so fast. Since then, Fil has refined the model, but his turnarounds are still from the same mold. The most telling point of all is that the plants and businesses that Fil has impacted upon continue to operate in line with his concepts and strategies.

Jim Chavalas
President
Cal Crane & Equipment, Inc.
Tracy, California USA
I have known Fil Filipov for many years and consider him first and foremost a great friend! My wife, Angela, and I have enjoyed Fil and Veronique's company in many cities around the world. As an owner of a business, I admire Fil for his tremendous dedication to business and great successes. His 100-day plan once a company is acquired is unsurpassed by any I have ever seen. It works! Fil is in the same category as Lee Iacocca, Donald Trump and Bill Gates: a winner!

QUALITY AND TURNAROUNDS

Dale Stoddard
Potain Corporation
Miami, Florida USA

The impact of Fil Filipov's and Terex's approach toward manufacturing and the industry has been profound. I would compare it to the impact that Japanese automobile manufacturers had on quality and customer preferences in the 1970s and early 1980s. First they ignored him, then they criticized him, and then they reacted to him. He has caused manufacturers, distributors and customers to reflect on their approach to the standard business models in their market segments and verify their approach, in many instances causing them to make major shifts in their organizations and product offerings in an effort to remain competitive.

His predatory approach toward gaining market share through cost reductions and offering basic products and services has severely impacted the profitability of many established market leaders in the industry. Most manufacturers have reorganized their production, marketing, administrative and sales organizations to offer a "Fil Light" version of his operational strategy, which has been generally beneficial to the overall marketplace by holding prices down. The pressure on prices has also had a negative effect on the market by reducing the level of service provided by manufacturers and distributors to the customer as the margins available do not provide sufficient capital to fund these services at "pre-Fil" levels.

As with all strategies, remaining stagnant and resisting change as the market dynamics change, will also have an influence on the overall impact of Fil's approach specifically as it relates to resale values of late model products. This is especially true for the large fleet owner who depends on lower than market acquisition prices and price increases in relation to their fleet value to fuel profitable sales of used equipment to fund new purchases.

Good, bad or indifferent, you would be hard pressed to find someone in the lifting business who has not heard of Fil Filipov.

FIL FILIPOV: FILOSOPHIES

John Irvine
General Manager
Cedarapids, Inc.
A Unit of Terex Earthmoving
Cedar Rapids, Iowa USA

I learned more working for Fil Filipov in the first three months than I had from my previous employer in the past 12 years. Fil is an accomplished business executive with phenomenal bottom-line focus. He relates to people in any environment due to his diverse background.

He sees problems through his employees eyes (good listener). His reputation as a hard driver is warranted. Seventy – 80-hour work weeks are common for Fil. He truly "walks the talk." He expects a great deal and gets results. He is passionate about his business. He is compassionate about his people and definitely his family.

A great leader, strict delegator, visionary, model figurehead, excellent disseminator of information is how I would sum up Fil Filipov.

Fil creates teamwork by stretching all his organizations to share resources and work together. You never feel like you work for a big company when you work for Fil. Everyone of your peers is someone you can trust and lean on in Fil's organization.

Fil's most impressive attribute is his ability to drive the most complex business problem to a "simple" solution quicker than anyone I know. He lives his Filosophy.

Equipment manufacture is his game, cost reduction is his fame.

QUALITY AND TURNAROUNDS

DO'S AND DON'TS
DURING RESTRUCTURING PERIODS

"Leaders are students of the past, critics of the present, and lovers of the future"

No Compromise

When you feel you are right do not let others talk you into something you do not believe in.

No Patterns

Do not do the same thing every day. Do not go to work at the same time each day, do not go to the shop the same time. Do things differently each day. People will get to know your patterns and can predict what you will do next.

No Problems

Do not let people dump problems on you to be solved. It is OK for them to make you aware of problems, but they must have solutions. If they do not have solutions, their problems become your problems.

No Closeness

Do not get close to the people. Restructuring periods are just that. They are not times when you are looking to get close to people. People will try to get close to you and get on your side for protection. There are no rules during these periods.

No Group Punishments

Treat problems on their own – do not punish the performers because you lack the guts to go after the ones that do not do their jobs.

No Promises

Do not make promises. For example, do not tell people if you do this, I will do this or allow you to do something special. You reward based upon performance and not upon promises.

No Friends

There is no time for friends when a business is being restructured. People are afraid of losing their jobs and will want to be your friend. There will be plenty of time for friends when the job is done.

Follow-up Yourself

Do not just push it down the ranks. Do the follow-up yourself.

Cheat Sheets
Write it down to free up your mind and use it all the time.
Be Brief
Conversations and instructions need to be short and clear. Too much conversation leads to confusion or misunderstanding.
THINK
You must take time each day to stop and think about what has happened during the day and what needs to be done during the remainder of he day. Not enough people take time to actually stop and think. Think before you act.

Decision making is not just an analysis of facts. There is a strong element of "gut feel" in the process and that is where experience plays an important role. Peter Drucker once said: "The importance of decision is not the money involved, but how fast the decision can be reversed if it is the wrong decision."

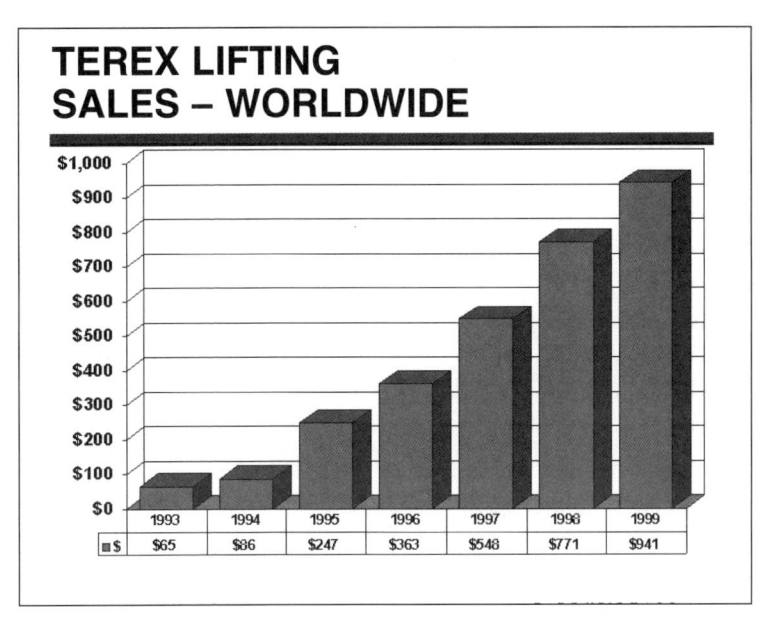

QUALITY AND TURNAROUNDS

TEREX LIFTING SALES – WORLDWIDE

	1993	1994	1995	1996	1997	1998	1999
$	$65	$86	$247	$363	$548	$771	$941

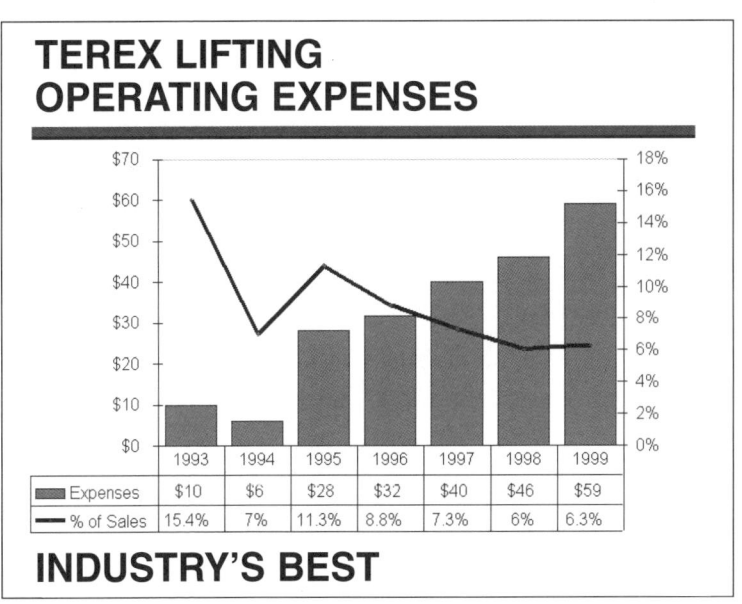

TEREX LIFTING OPERATING EXPENSES

	1993	1994	1995	1996	1997	1998	1999
Expenses	$10	$6	$28	$32	$40	$46	$59
% of Sales	15.4%	7%	11.3%	8.8%	7.3%	6%	6.3%

INDUSTRY'S BEST

TEREX LIFTING OPERATING PROFIT

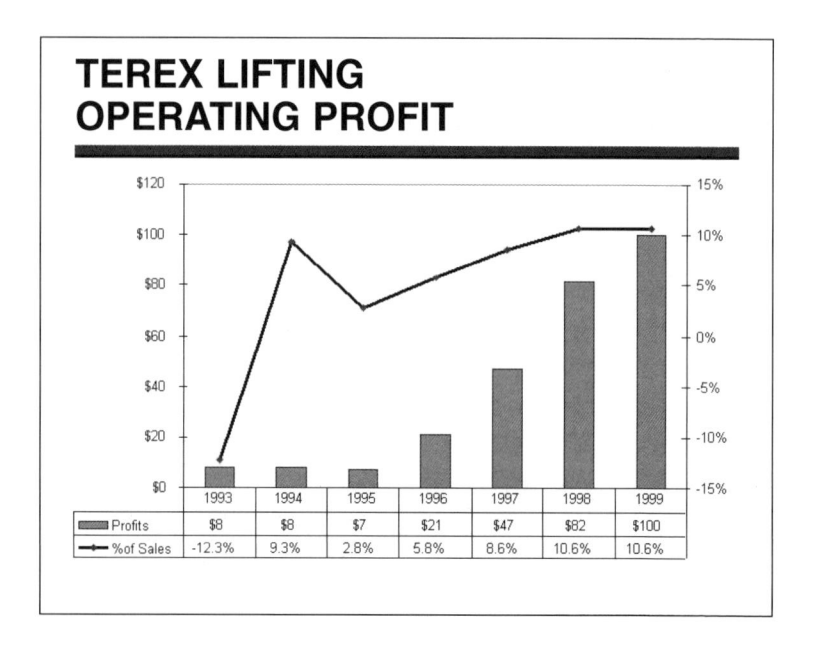

	1993	1994	1995	1996	1997	1998	1999
Profits	$8	$8	$7	$21	$47	$82	$100
% of Sales	-12.3%	9.3%	2.8%	5.8%	8.6%	10.6%	10.6%

VII
BASIC BELIEFS – THE EIGHT M'S

There are eight fundamental principals I have compiled through my business experiences and adhered to with remarkable success. I call them my "Eight M's" and they are: Manpower, Money, Material, Machines, Markets, Motivation, Morale and Management.

Manpower
A steady diet of hard work does not kill; it makes me live longer and happier. People will make or break the business. When it comes to the time to reduce the headcount, I make a plea for a more humane handling of downsizing. By keeping a constant eye on the headcount, direct versus indirect ratios, productivity, efficiency, outsourcing, cost-per-hour and fringe benefits, you can find the "sweet spot" where the perfect number of employees helps the business perform best.

Money
What is a business in the final analysis? The answer of course is money! Most companies can reduce costs by 30 to 50 percent by doing a few simple things; Refuse to accept price increases and re-evaluate commissions and bonuses. Take control of expense reports, reduce phone charges, reduce part numbers and optimize insurance coverage. We need to remember, (receiv-

ables+inventory)-payables = working capital.

Material
Like it or not, good housekeeping is essential for quality and efficiency. Not enough people give credit to the adage "a place for everything and everything in its place." Material is money. Do you have just in time or just in case? How high are your part numbers?

Machines
Finished machines are to be sold. Office machines are to help make the sale. Do not let people sell you things that you do not need.

Markets
Practice new methods of broadening the markets. Avoid exclusive distribution. Offer price advantages. Take time to understand market share and what it really means. Look at statistics, observations and ways to diagnose performance in the marketplace. Then get out there and take it away from your competitors. Do whatever it takes. What does the order book look like?

Motivation
What is the bottom line? Business is a web of uncertainty. It's a network of diverse problems and complex interdependencies which we must manage by continually spinning a revising agenda and by keeping tight control of day-to-day operations. Our people must want to work with us. No bureaucracies help contribute to constant motivation improvements.

Morale
Whether there's a risk involved, a move to make or a decision that must be made quickly, we must make things happen.

BASIC BELIEFS – THE EIGHT M'S

Morale often hinges on quickly setting clear objectives to respond to changes in the business environment. Those who believe in you will go the extra mile. The rest get in the way.

Management
Nothing makes for success in business like a sense of urgency. Leadership involves breathing, eating and sleeping while creating our own "artificial" deadlines with room to make mistakes. Elegance and executive bearing aside, business is basically a boxing match. When boxing, fans and media love the spectacular blows to he head. But what really wins the match is a constant job, jab, jab at the opponent's body.

Some punches will get blocked, some will miss entirely. But if you take aim at the biggest target you can see, and do your best to pound on it persistently, you will win! Every match may not be a knockout. The match may not be over in the second round, but eventually you will win!

A truly successful business in this global environment cannot stand still for a lot of formal theories, empowered networking and consciousness-raising long meetings. While you are trying to get your act together and embrace some new theory, your competitors are punching you where it hurts. In order to be successful, you have to stay in the ring and keep punching day in and day out.

When writing a book like this, it's easy to slip into writing a how-to manual. We've all seen them: action plans, flowcharts and magic formulas offered by so-called experts or consultants promising immediate and dramatic results. Usually, the only one who profits is the writer. That is not my goal. My objectives are to inspire thought and action. As a maverick all my life, I prefer to expose a simpler way of managing business, and a simpler way of living. That isn't really something a how-to manual can do. I may disappoint the competition because no trade secrets are given here, but it takes guts to do what I had to do and move forward.

There are three kinds of people in the world: those who don't have a clue what is happening, those who watch things happen and those who make things happen, otherwise known as leaders or winners.

Those who don't have a clue just want to collect a paycheck. They drift aimlessly from job to job, from task to task with no sense of purpose, no enthusiasm, no sense of challenge and making little or no contribution.

The people that watch things happen make whining a national sport. They cruise through life, letting somebody else carry most of the load. When nobody shows up to meet their expectations, they fret, fuss, complain and generally make a nuisance of themselves. Their excuses are rampant. "It's the market." "It's the economy." "It's the product." "It's the ..." Rarely do they take action. These excuse-mongers devastate morale and the bottom line.

Winners drive for results. Leaders stand right at the front and hold onto the reins. At times disliked, and some may dismiss them as harsh, hyperactive or control freaks, they get the job done. Success in business comes from taking focused action. It is not a by-product of genius, although it helps a lot to know what you're doing; of passion, although believing in something is critical; or by constantly re-organizing the business. Success comes to those with their sleeves at their elbows and their mind on their work. People who meet life at the gate and wrestle it to the ground may be hard to take sometimes, but they make things happen. Every action contributes toward the objective – whatever that may be.

Losers count the damages. They may wake up and realize missed opportunities, but such a revelation is rare. Losers usually fall in the "success is a journey" group. Success is no such thing. It's related to the ability to control the events of life. Losers spend far too much time trying to minimize problems and avoid pain, rather than stand up to the challenge and take it on the chin. It's okay to win. We can have the most wonderful intentions, use the best systems, follow expert guidelines, manage time down to the second and money down to the penny, but if we don't get results, none of that means anything. Let me say it again, a little louder: RESULTS ARE ALL THAT COUNT.

Winners think hard and think often. Many people are lazy, not only in the sense of work, but also in the use of their brains. They allow their minds to wander, letting whatever random thoughts or emotions pop into their heads and disrupt whatever they are doing at the moment. I set aside time to do nothing but think, and I guarantee that done correctly, it's the hardest work one has ever done. So many people get to the end of the day and can't go to sleep, mainly because they just haven't worked hard enough. Let's be honest: Most of us probably spend a great deal of time behind a desk or doing our work sitting in a chair. If that's true, we certainly aren't going to tire ourselves out due to physical exertion – that is, we aren't working hard from the perspective of a mason who carries bricks up a ladder. To produce a similar level of effort, we have to be thinking all the time – all the time.

Losers let other people do the thinking. It baffles me that so many companies blindly accept procedures, practices and ideas touted by academics and high-priced consultants. Why would someone take the word of a professor who's never spent a day outside the classroom, or trust a person whose only claim to fame is a series of thick, expensive books on business? What do they know? The answer is absolutely nothing. Consultants take our wallet, count the money we have in it, then take half of it and inform us that we do not have enough.

I am living proof that a successful business can be run with amazing simplicity, without all those procedures, policies and theories that tie people's hands and give managers an excuse for not doing anything. But I also have the personal experience to draw on. Do the homework and think, if a consultant is needed, find a business person who has been a success in the real world and can be brutally honest with you. (Pay before receiving the advice!) We may not like it, but it's the only way to snap out of your funk.

Winners learn from their past but always move forward. One of the most influential moments of my life was in the refugee camp in Greece. A fellow prisoner spoke very good English, although no one knew why. What we did know was that this middle-aged man was actually in camp for the second time. After I obtained a sewing machine and started to repair the Salvation Army's monthly clothes giveaways, he came to my "shop" one day and started talking to me like a friend. He told me about his escape from Communist Bulgaria some 15 years earlier, emmigrating to New Zealand where he got married. Years later, his wife left with his best friend. Depressed, he decided to return to Bulgaria – a huge mistake. Six years later, risking his life, he escaped again. He did not know where to go, but that really didn't matter to him. Despite the hardship brought on by communism and a broken marriage, he was determined not to worry about the past or use it as an excuse. It's an attitude everyone should have. Do not look back – look forward and be positive.

Losers look for excuses. They blame their parents, their spouse, the lack of opportunity, bad luck, or one of a thousand other excuses. Nobody told them this was life. Nobody told them they would need to be responsible for their own success. Mostly they are caught up in permanent "neg-ativism."

The United States Military Academy has an excellent approach to handling whining. For their entire first year, a cadet can give only four answers to anything: "Yes," "No," "I don't understand," and "No excuse." This may seem harsh to some people, but it's a perfectly valid way to operate, and one that would do many companies good to emulate. When we agree to take on a responsibility, or see something that must be changed, we must change it.

Arriving at the refugee camp, I was quite surprised to see hundreds of people from other communist countries, including some as far away as Cuba, who had escaped hiding in a ship. I was one of the youngest members of this group and could not help but notice how negative most people were. Here we are – having just escaped communism, destined for a better life and people were complaining about the food!

Some companies spend an awful lot of time making excuses these days. One of the most prevalent methods of whining in corporate America today is the "reorganization." Some of the largest companies in the country reorganize multiple times a year. Sometimes it's because of poor results, but usually it's because it gives them something to blame for their lack of profitability. I believe in reorganization, but do it once and do it according to who's getting the job done, and not to satisfy popular trends. I could go into almost any of these companies and cut overhead by 50 percent as well as improve products and quality and double their profits within nine months. This is what I do best: I am very good at bad times. I'm not ashamed of it, and to tell the truth, I enjoy it. There are doctors and there are surgeons. I have grown to be a good surgeon compared to some so-called restructuring specialists.

The most obvious reason I do not advocate how-to manuals is that everyone does things differently. You and I may agree that hard work is essential, that no one should consider themselves indispensable and that honesty is essential, but our individual situations and the way we implement these ideas, however, will vary so much that any more specific advice I might give is probably meaningless.

FILOSOPHY – THE 8 M'S

- MANPOWER
- MONEY
- MATERIAL
- MARKETS
- MACHINES
- MOTIVATION
- MORALE
- MANAGEMENT

Winners drive for results.
Losers count the damages.
Whiners look for excuses.

SUCCESS IN BUSINESS COMES FROM TAKING FOCUSED ACTIONS

BASIC BELIEFS – THE EIGHT M'S

General Managers
Check List

Look for ways to improve productivity.

How to improve the top 10 quality problems.

Inventory reduction plan for top 50 highest cost items.

Go to receiving and improve on lot quantity, packaging, transportation.

Ways to in – or outsource to improve material handling and flow.

Purchase subassembies for cost and vendor reductions.

Are machine tools utilized?

Finish machines status.

Burden material – consumables. Any excess? Call and ask for cost reductions.

Accounts receivable – held up due to quality?

Visit wash rooms – are they clean?

Safety and working conditions?

Air tools – do you hear their utilization?

Check on paint/prepainted method change.

Status on new product prototypes.

Visit the yard – do not avoid visiting places! Any places!

Go check on one or two items of your recent employee survey.

Consider and make changes – get people on the shop floor from the offices.

FIL FILIPOV: FILOSOPHIES

VIII
TAKING CHARGE AND LEADING

Truly managing change. Driving for excellence. Pleasing customers with a product that is *Simple, Available and Cost Effective*. Capturing the loyalty of employees. I put these most-important characteristics together – as well as make more profit for the company and more income for myself.

Leadership means side-stepping trendy, unproven management philosophies and resisting the urge to chase the easy buck. Leadership requires hard work and thinking on my own. The words of Ralph Waldo Emerson still ring true: " ... that envy is ignorance; that imitation is suicide; that no kernel of nourishing corn can come to us, except by our own hand."

On one side, there are success systems that encourage us to set our heart on a small group of goals and then plow forward relentlessly and mindlessly, grinding ourselves into sand in reaching them. Don't get me wrong: I'm a big believer in clear goals and hard work. But there's a difference between focused action and beating your head against a wall. There's also a difference between simplicity of purpose and single-mindedness. If you are blindly obsessed with goals, what happens when hidden doors open, offering new opportunities? Will you refuse to walk through simply because it isn't in the mission statement?

At the other end of the spectrum are approaches that teach us to wander with the winds, relying on fate to provide whatever needed and exactly when needed. Success is looked upon as a journey, something to be enjoyed. Yes, there is something intensely spiritual about events that seem to work themselves out – but strolling aimlessly and mindlessly through life makes those gifts of Providence a desperate necessity, rather than a reward for hard-earned results.

The truth, as always, is somewhere in between. An old proverb reminds us, "Take life the way it happens, but try to make it happen the way you want to take it." To expect cold logic to solve every problem is as much superstition as holding out a hungry hand and waiting for an apple to fall into it. By the same token, only fools expect success without putting a hand on the tiller.

STYLISTIC SELF-LEADERSHIP

Much has been made of leadership "styles" – a person's specific way of dealing with people and events to produce a result. Business authors have slapped labels on dozens, perhaps hundreds, of styles, but I believe there are basically three types: bureaucratic, enlightened and active.

Bureaucratic leadership seems to be most concerned with satisfying everyone at the cost of progress, creating a compromise that balances natural human resistance to change with risk-taking. Team consensus rules, often regardless of the objectives. Facts become perspectives, perspectives become "just one man's opinion," and opinions become issues that will neither die nor get off the table. Centering around the idea of keeping everyone happy, this style often diffuses effort and blunts the impact of any one action upon the total result, slowing progress.

Enlightened leadership, on the other hand, seems to express a "life as an indivisible whole" philosophy, a sort of family-as-community flavor that offers a set of underlying values upon which decisions are based. Higher purposes are carefully defined to assure that even the most decisive actions bring meaning and fulfillment through the work itself, without placing very much emphasis on results. Such leadership carries a hierarchy of ideas, beginning with a mission statement that provides an overall sense of purpose, intended to permeate every aspect of the workplace. The most difficult task in this environment is maintaining integrity – that is, keeping actions in line with values. Unfortunately, there is an inherent disparity that enlightened leadership creates between value-centered goals and healthy self-interest. You cannot, for example, translate a goal of contributing to society into giving away your house and putting your family on the street. No matter what our values, we must grow in all dimensions, and any approach that does not take this into consideration is not realistic.

Active leadership represents a third clear style, built upon the premise that "action is better than reaction." People who practice this method make a point of setting clear, specific, realistic goals which deal directly with both short and long-term realities and observable dynamics, not happy abstractions or objectives that are "good for all of mankind," although mankind may indeed benefit from the results. These leaders are self-motivated and willing to take personal responsibility for outcomes. If necessary, they are prepared to risk mediocre rewards and initiate major changes to achieve their goals. Decisions are based upon facts that can be verified, strategy evolves from high standards and simple reasoning, and people are motivated with a combination of pressure and inspiration drawn from an honest assessment of conditions and potential. At its very core, this style recognizes that a company must make a profit to stay in business, and that a person must grow to stay happy.

FIL FILIPOV: FILOSOPHIES

FOCUSING ON RESULTS

Unfortunately, however, none of these three styles adequately captures the sometimes intuitive, always consciously-chosen path that a leader must take to guarantee profitable growth and fulfillment, or that a company must take to ensure market share. The process of successful living is like a long hike through the woods, compass in hand. You know you're headed in a northerly direction, but the exact path and destination depend upon skills, the changes going on in the world and the opportunities that come up along the way. Active leadership would take an absolute straight line to the pre-defined goal, cutting down trees and clearing bush in the process. While this might be the most efficient way to get there, it isn't always the most effective, and it destroys valuable assets in the process – not to mention the fact that you might get to the clearing and find out that everyone else went the other way.

Bureaucratic leadership would take no steps without first assuring the consensus of the group, so progress depends directly upon the competence and solidarity of purpose of many people. In a highly cohesive family or business unit, rapid progress is not out of the question, but the typical team would probably linger in the woods until they heard the wolves howl and then run madly in all directions, seeking the nearest moon-lit trail – where they end up is anybody's guess.

Finally, enlightened leadership would encourage everyone to enjoy the woods as they are passing through, and perhaps they would find a way to make a significant profit serving others who are traveling there, never even attempting to leave the forest.

While each of these methods provides value, none of them really address the fundamental issue – coming out of the woods at just the right time, at the perfect spot (though perhaps not the original destination), flexing around the inevitable obstacles in the landscape, and taking advantage of the natural assets of the environment, having grown as much as possible in the process. In short, creating a flowing and unpredictable synergy with change: adapting to it, redirecting it, embracing it, but always responding to it, and always moving as close as possible to a direction of your own choosing. Set the course for the far horizon, without failing to enjoy the beauty of the journey, always ready to change direction and recognize opportunity 10 degrees left of the line on the chart.

IMPROVING INDIVIDUAL LEADERSHIP

Our business simply reflects ourselves: Playing to images portrayed in the media and chasing dreams that are in direct opposition to one another, we become frustrated and disappointed with the way our lives are working out. In the space of only one day, the average person must adopt 20-30 roles, constantly dropping one set of values and picking up another in an effort to present the best face (and presumably get the most out of) every situation. The resulting lack of integrity leaves us feeling depressed, confused and terminally out of sync with reality. Our lists of goals and things to do are often so extensive that if we spend only one minute each on the truly important ones alone, we would need another 12 hours in the day. Our constant sense of missing something only intensifies our feelings of disappointment and imminent woe.

In the world of business, as well as life, success and failure is often a matter of setting priorities and allocating time. With proper timing, we all can cherish the results that are consistent, positive and stimulating to the growth of the business. This means refraining from developing and becoming obsessed with grocery-store lists of five-, 10- and 20-year goals. Many people spend far too much time writing down their goals and far too little time seizing opportunity when it presents itself. If you are not keenly aware of your top seven or eight goals, if they do not drive what you do every single day – well, don't ask me for a job.

It all comes down to loving what you do. If you're only doing something for the money, you're not going to be very good at it. Better to take what you love to do and figure out how to make it pay off, then find a way to make a fortune working hard at it. How many people go through the time-consuming routine of writing down their goals and accomplishments in a daily planner? If you need paper to constantly remind yourself what's important, it's apparent you don't love what you do – and it's time to move on.

Leaders understand there is no substitute for hard work. That's the way it is and always will be. I am convinced that if you want something badly enough, you can do it, regardless of the obstacles or the official prerequisites for the job.

During the early stages of my management career, I enrolled in college thinking a degree would probably help me in some way at some time in my life. I felt that if you want something bad enough, you should be willing to do whatever is necessary to achieve it. So I started and then one day, someone told me that a college degree was an absolute must; that without it I would never get another promotion. Never, ever tell me it can't be done, because I will do everything in my power to prove you wrong. I dropped out of college and I have never returned.

Schools can teach us many things, but one thing they can't teach is how to be successful. To this day, every time I receive a promotion I make sure to send that individual a short note: "I did it again." I've mailed him a lot of letters over the years.

IX
THEY CAN HANDLE THE TRUTH

Of the few management books I have read, all have stressed the importance of communication – the external variety to customers, and within the organization to employees. Frequent and honest communication helps keep customers happy and inspires employees to contribute. So why do so many executives have trouble with this concept, sharing no useful information at all or issuing rambling, management-speak speeches or press releases that leave customers and employees asking, "What was that about?"

Let's not kid ourselves: Hiding things or trying to pull the wool over somebody's eyes rarely works, and even when it does it's only a matter of time until the truth comes to the surface. When it comes to communication, I am honest, thorough, clear, quick, and try to do the impossible: Beat the grapevine. This requires thinking through the scenarios in advance. During my morning shower, I think through my day in advance, preparing myself for what's coming. When things do happen, I can communicate accurately and immediately, which lends power to what I have to say. This applies whether I communicate with customers, suppliers, partners, competitors, employees, bosses or the media.

Two-way communication with the customer happens not once a quarter, not once a week, not a few days after a product has been introduced. It takes place on a daily basis. The question of customer satisfaction is my No. 1 priority, which makes communication a natural instinct. Where is my sales force? What are they selling? How much are they selling? How and where am I meeting the markets? Do I know what my customers need? How much do they want to spend and what are the economic conditions behind their decisions? I could go on with a list of questions for 30 pages, but you get the idea. On a daily basis, there is always something new to learn about the markets, the customers and the distribution channels we are using.

The "Available" part of *Simple, Available and Cost Effective* refers not only to the product but also to yourself. Executives and managers must be available to field all customer calls, and I do mean all. Meetings, presentations, politics and anything else that takes you from the customer should be kept to a minimum. Nothing, absolutely nothing is more important than making sure customers are satisfied. When I make a customer contact, I always try to follow up as quickly as possible. Even if I do not have much to share, I call the people to let them know, "I'm working on it," that I am keenly aware of their problem and taking direct responsibility for its solution. One big mistake is leaving customer issues hanging for days, letting them float until they crash into the rocks and the customer decides to do business elsewhere. The customer pays for a product and expects a response, so I keep in mind there is always an answer to the question – find it and follow up on it. We must be available. I at times call and look for myself. Try it yourself and see how the customer feels.

Managers and salespeople are not the only players when it comes to staying in touch with the customer. The administrative assistants – or receptionists – play a critical role. Taking phone calls, welcoming visitors, they influence the customers' first impression of each encounter with the company. Receptionists who do their job well are often the most productive people in the organization. They answer every call with courtesy, respect and speed, at times acting as the sounding board for irritated customers and unraveling complicated conversations to figure out how to route the call. I select these individuals carefully, train them completely and pay them very well – much more than most companies would ever consider. I also give them other responsibilities so they can build their skills and get a break from the monotony of a single task. Do not overlook their importance.

Allow me to offer another suggestion on customer communications: I refrain from falling into the trap of voicemail. The beauty of the telephone is that it allows for immediate communication. By calling someone, you presumably want to talk to the person right away, otherwise you would have sent them a letter or an overnight package. Now with voicemail, some business people regard their phone system as just another set of mail boxes, where customers are directed to leave messages and basically left hanging not knowing when or if their calls will be returned. Is the person really not in the office, or are you simply being avoided? Leaving a message on a person's voicemail, they call back and get your voicemail, you call back and get their voicemail. Talk about exasperating. This is supposed to help communications?

The same goes for these "push one" systems. Nothing is more irritating than hacking our way through five levels of directions, thinking we are eventually going to reach someone, only to be asked to leave a voicemail because the person we need to speak with is unavailable. Or worse, be put on hold for 20 minutes waiting for the "next available representative." This is customer service at its worst. Reasonable people will take their business elsewhere. I will never allow the use of voice-menu systems used this way at any company I run.

I use voicemail like an old-fashioned answering machine. If

I'm at my desk, I answer the phone. It's that simple. If my customers are directed to leave a message, they know I will get back to them as soon as I can. They also know I am more than happy to take their calls during off-hours. I pride myself on being one of the most accessible executives in the business

When talking on the phone, my goal is to keep the conversation clear and concise; in another word, efficient. If a specific subject needs to be discussed, think it through beforehand so nobody's time is wasted. This approach may sound gruff, but business discussions should be short and to the point so both parties can get back to work. Save the casual stuff for the restaurant or golf course.

COMMUNICATION WITHIN THE ORGANIZATION

If we want our employees to go to war for us, to understand and embrace our strategy and, most importantly, produce results, we have to tell them like it is. They can handle the truth. In most instances, they want the truth.

Motivation is impossible if clear objectives are not communicated down to the lowest levels. Most companies don't take this approach out of fear. Their concern is if employees are told the product is not selling well or that a key customer has pulled its business, they might leave and go somewhere else. Sharing good news, such as capturing a huge order, is also frowned upon because employees might ask for a raise. It is commonly thought that keeping the staff guessing about the state of the business is the best way to maintain control, when in fact, most of the time, the employees will make the discovery on their own.

In times of prosperity and despair – and every condition in between – honest communication is the only option. No matter how hard we try to sugar-coat a bad situation, employees will see through it, become distrustful and lose respect. Credibility is damaged if not destroyed. I do much better when I convey a deep sense of urgency and express my real concerns over problems. If things are going well, a sincere thank you and a firm handshake is all that's needed – people know when you mean it. They deserve the truth, no matter how bad or good it might be at the moment.

Some who have worked for me probably think I can be maniacal when it comes to communication. I publicize in-house our bills for computer hardware and software, utilities, telephone service, even property taxes, drilling down to the per-day cost. I regularly emphasize the themes of hard work, organization (a place for everything and everything in its place) and commitment to excellence. Again, my approach is blunt, but honest and to the point. There is no room for misinterpretation. Here are two examples of my messages:

TO ALL EMPLOYEES: Anything is possible – with practice. The successful are those who overcome all temptation not to work hard. They labor without complaint. They get results. Excellence is produced by hard work, not by excuses.

TO ALL EMPLOYEES: July was a terrible month! It is now history and we can do nothing about it. SOME of you need to worker harder to make August the beginning of OUR turnaround. The Terex staff meeting will be held here August 19-20. We need the place to be presentable. I am counting on you! (The August production objectives then follow.)

Of course, the written word by itself does not motivate or help morale. On the contrary, it de-motivates because without the face-to-face contact to back it up, it comes off as fake and contemptuous. That's why Management by Walking Around (MBWA) is so important. Employees in all parts of an organization, and in particular the people on the floor (remember, I was one of them), want to see and hear, not just read, what their boss is all about. An executive who is visible, genuine and engages in spontaneous discussions with his or her employees will experience far greater success than the boss huddled in the office. It not only inspires loyalty from the work force, but I can pick up some interesting facts that managers have been hesitant to share. When making my rounds, I am forthcoming, present my message and tell the truth. Lies and misrepresentations will come back and bite you later.

I speak the truth up as well as down the chain of command. I try to tell my boss things that he needs to know, things that will help him make better decisions. We all have bosses. I have always wanted to be the Pope because his boss is the farthest away. It's no different than the approach I use with my employees and my customers. We talk when we need to talk about issues pertinent to the bottom line. Too many people sit around the office, waiting for that important call from the boss, rather than visiting a customer or addressing a problem in the plant. Let the boss find me. If your boss needs to know everything all the time, it's time to get a new boss. On the flip side, if someone you supervise keeps calling you, watch out! The person is probably trying to establish a cozy relationship before dropping the bomb that results are not being achieved. Stay focused on the objective and keep me informed about progress – no news is good news – but don't call me with revised forecasts because yesterday was a bad day or you want assurances that I still like you.

Communication can get out of hand. Most meetings, for example are a waste of time. A common problem with meetings is that there's too much on the agenda, with too little time for substantive discussion and action. If you must have a meeting, focus exactly on one well-defined subject.

I try to communicate with a purpose. It does not matter if I am speaking at a policyholder's meeting, talking one-on-one with a customer or writing a short memo to employees. I make sure my message is clear, concise and meaningful. Remember, I want to inspire trust and, in many cases, immediate action. Take it from a person who's gone through it many times. If you want to change a losing behavior, if you want to reverse the fortunes of a struggling company, you must communicate your expectations early and often. You will not achieve results with jargon, half-truths and ambiguity. Some of our employees may not be happy with what we have to say – yes, some may even leave because of it – but those who stay, and the organization as a whole, will be much better off in the long term.

FIL FILIPOV: FILOSOPHIES

X
MY SUPPORT GROUP

Sitting back in Chicago in his 47th floor home office looking down on the city's famed Magnificent Mile, the refugee again contemplates his journey.

Thirty-four years later, he is only a few blocks away from his first job in industry but how things have changed – as he says, he now takes a cab instead of a bus ... can afford more expensive earmuffs ... enjoys a life style that is light years away from the most humble and lonely levels in which he entered the business world. Drinking from a cup carrying the NO WHINING sign on it, he reflects.

I have learned a lot and found life to be the best teacher. My life has changed and so much for the better. Much has been accomplished, but a lot of the credit has to go to others that have had such a positive influence on my life and the way I live it.

They say a loving atmosphere in your home is the foundation for your life. Veronique has provided that base and has respected my business and personal friends.

I tell people I am Vero's husband rather than she is my wife. People will say I'm the guy with the young French wife. That is true, but she is so much more. To me, she is the most important part of my personal and business life and turnaround process. They also say that a man without a good wife cannot be happy and successful. I have found the partner I need.

From experience I know that as early as age 40 women

often try to find themselves. I keep thinking that with Vero, if this were to happen, I have a few more years to go. I sincerely hope nothing is forever does not apply here.

Veronique Filipov
It is difficult to talk about my husband and be objective in just a few words, but I will try. When he asked me to say a few things about him, I think he forgot for a moment that I was French and, as he has repeated so many times, when you ask a French person what time it is, they want to tell you how to make the watch. I will stay true to my French origin.

I met Fil more than 10 years ago in France. Even before I learned his name, I experienced his affinity for taking risks. "Don't fall in love with me," he said with a flirtatious smile. Fortunately, for both of us I did not heed his half-hearted warning, even though I am 18 years his junior.

Since the day we met, life has been an adventure. We have shared exciting experiences, some good and some bad. Yet through it all, and no matter what the situation or location, Fil has remained true to his principles. He works incredibly hard, but he demands no less from himself than he does from anyone else.

I will leave the professional judgment to others. Let me speak only for the man I know as "Fifo." He is my husband, my best friend, my lover and my confidant. He tells people he has made five major decisions in his life: leave his home country, divorce after 22 years, separate from a 25-year career with Case, quit smoking and marry a much younger woman. I am proud to be such an important part of his life.

Fil has never forgotten his heritage. He always says, "Remember where you came from, keep your feet on the ground, and don't get a big head." In his heart he is still a refugee. He preaches unpredictability but I can read his mind because he is so superstitious. There are times I don't know where our next trip will take us, but I always know on what side of the bed I will sleep – for Fil makes sure he begins each day on the right foot, literally and figuratively.

MY SUPPORT GROUP

Fil and Veronique Filipov, Switzerland, 1992.

From the beginning, we had to make major decisions about our lifestyle and our priorities. Some people may view us selfish and I must admit that in some instances we probably are. Together, we have no children. When my mother asked us for a grandchild, Fil – true to form – jokingly introduced her to Steve, his 25-year-old son.

I think it is important for a wife to be knowledgeable about her husband's career, and I have a good understanding of Fil's business. I know the people he works with, as well as many of his customers. We discuss his trials and tribulations, but I leave the business decisions to him. He always says the wife makes the couple, but I think it takes two to make a marriage work. We have been fortunate not to have an argument during our relationship. But let me be honest, we do not have three of the major concerns that start family arguments – children, money and career. While there may be no such thing as a perfect marriage, ours is pretty close.

Fil and I have spent many wonderful years together and I have learned so many things – I am still learning. Nothing is forever, and nothing is easy. I remember having to face the decision to leave France and move to the United States with Fil. I knew nothing of our destination, Waverly, Iowa, or what I was going to do when I got there. It would mean starting over: new home, new friends, new language, essentially a brand new way of life. Yet, it really didn't matter because I was with Fil. If I was going to be a part of his life, I was determined to be part of the solution and not the problem.

It was my turn to become an expatriate, just as Fil had been at other times of his life. He had succeeded in France and I wanted to do as well in the United States. Iowa was the perfect place. We made friends and we enjoyed our stay, but when you are a Filipov, you know any stay is temporary. It's a place to stop before the next move. I must say we are looking forward to returning to France someday and watching the vineyards grow in Burgundy.

The Fil I know is much more than a driven leader. In addition to being a caring, supportive husband, he has friends around the world, with some of those relationships now more than 30 years old. I marvel at his generosity and eagerness to do whatever he can to help those close to him.

The years we have spent together have been wonderful and I am always learning. And for the people who ask if I am bored, please let me assure you I am not. Taking care of Fil is anything but boring. As I've said before, my life with him is an adventure and is just beginning...

Our home is always open to our friends. Good cooking and French wine are our secrets.

One of the most satisfying parts of a man's life is to see a son follow in his footsteps – to see him find his way and progress to the point where he has the competence and self assurance to tackle tough situations and resolve them.

I'm sure my son, Steve, had to think long and hard before deciding to join me at Terex Lifting. He was well aware of my standards, my work ethic and my expectations of everyone around me. And he knew he would be measured the same way

MY SUPPORT GROUP

– the only way – and that is by performance. And perform he has at a level far beyond what can be expected for his age. He has made me very proud.

Steve Filipov

Who is Fil Filipov? In a strict professional sense, words that immediately come to mind are diligent, focused, relentless and confident. I have been blessed because my experiences with him go far beyond the business world. I am his son. He is my "Tatko."

What astonishes me most about my father is his incredible amount of energy. He is a person always on the move, always thinking about his next step – not only for himself but also for the people around him. We have worked together for 10 years now and we've been through some rough times, but he has never let anything get him down. Some people may wonder, "How do you do it? How can you stick with Fil Filipov, albeit he is your father, for 32 years?" The truth is I have no regrets, and I would not change a thing. I learn something new every day I work with him.

Let me share some of the stories and the lessons I have learned. Some may seem harsh and some are humorous, but all have made lasting impressions and contributed to who I am today. Looking back, I was so lucky to have these moments with my father. I can only hope I can share similar experiences with my children.

I remember that first learning experience as if it happened yesterday. It was a lesson on the importance of being independent, on relying on yourself. We had recently moved from Kentucky half way across the world to Paris, France. I was 12 years old and spoke like a Southern bluegrass farmer. I knew only two words in French, "oui" and "non." One morning in August, at about 6 a.m., my father woke me up and said he wanted to show me – actually, tell me – how to get to school.

"Here's your monthly pass for the bus and metro," he said. "You get on bus number 10, get off at Porte d'Auteuil, go down to the metro, catch the line to Gare d'Austerlitz, and get off at the stop Emile Zola.

FIL FILIPOV: FILOSOPHIES

Father and son in Conway, South Carolina, 1995.

When you come out, if you do not see the Eiffel Tower, you are lost. Ask directions or call me. Otherwise walk 500 meters and there you are, at school. No problem."

All that for a little boy who knew two words in French. The first weeks were tough and I probably hated him for it, but by the end of the first month not only was I the pro of the Parisian transportation network, but fluent in French. Moral of the story? Well, there were several: Don't be afraid of the unknown, have a target, face and conquer your fears, appreciate and learn from different cultures, and know how to ask for help when you need it.

Many teens on the verge of adulthood think they know everything and don't listen to anyone, especially their father. After moving from France to Belgium, where my father continued his steady climb to the top, I returned to the United States to attend college. I then moved to Texas to work for a trading company that was owned by another refugee from Eastern Europe, a Hungarian by the name of Gabi. I learned a lot from Gabi. In a sense, he was my spiritual father, and just like him I wanted to have my own business. But as I had learned four languages by then, I also wanted to go back to Europe. Here's where the fun began.

My father, who was working for J.I. Case at the time, said there was an opportunity for me to work there over the summer. I had heard from my friends that this was going to be great: Deliver mail, talk on the phone, do nothing and get paid. Boy, were they wrong! "Son, you're on the 5 a.m. shift on the finishing line, go get 'em," my father told me. Here I go, no experience, only the love of machines and oil. Well, the boys on the line had a test waiting for me – take off that hydraulic hose, put a new one on. I then learned, by the bath of hydraulic oil, that you must first break the seal, reduce the pressure and slowly change the hose, or else.

I stayed on the 5 a.m. shift for six weeks. I became proficient at welding and calibrating excavators, as well as performing final tests of machines. I also learned when Mr. Filipov passes through the shop you better be working or sweeping the floors, or else find another job. Still, the workers and my father shared a deep respect for each other. When they needed to talk to him, he would listen. When he asked for more productivity, the workers pushed, pulled, basically did everything they could to meet the goal.

Just as it was for my father 30 years earlier, my time on the line was invaluable. Not only did I learn lessons the hard way, I paid careful attention to how my father conducted himself and his business. (A place for everything; everything is place.) My father, in turn, watched me. An image I will always remember was when he walked through the shop with the chief executive officer of Case. I was sweeping the floors and my father pointed and said, "That's my son." He was proud, and that made me feel great. At that point, our relationship started to grow.

What happened next could fill up another book. While in France, I purchased a truck and every month loaded it with chocolates, diapers, yarn and anything else I could get my hands on. Then I drove 2,500 kilometers to Bulgaria and sold the inventory. Although the income was good, the back-and-forth treks were exhausting. Once in a while, I would get so tired I would sell everything – including the truck – just so I could fly home.

At the age of 22 came my first real test. Had I learned enough to take a struggling company, restructure it and turn it into a growing business? I will never forget when my father told me he needed some help in France. I would have 120 people and eight branches, and would have to let the current general manager go. I put a plan together to restructure the entire distribution system and submitted it to my father. I impatiently waited for his answer. He called me from Germany and said, "This is a Filipov plan. Looks good, now implement it." In six months the plan was implemented and we had grown the business by 20 percent.

I am extremely fortunate that my father and I have developed such a close relationship. There have been a lot of sacrifices, but they've been worth it. I am sure he will continue to surprise everybody with his energy and ideas. It takes a lot of guts nowadays to be different and show the world there are very simple ways to run a business, teach others, and have a successful career. But it takes perseverance.

Not only does he work hard to satisfy customers, but he tries just as hard to satisfy relatives and friends. How many fathers celebrate the marriage of their son and daughter-in-law with three weddings? My wife, Alexandra, and I were first married in Las Vegas in the same chapel as my father and his bride, Veronique, had wed. (My father told me to write down the address for the grandchildren). He always wants things short and to the point and the ceremony took all of three minutes.

Three months later we had a more traditional wedding at a distinguished castle close to Paris with cherished friends. The service was somewhat longer than the one in Las Vegas.

The third wedding was held in Plovdiv, Bulgaria, my father's home town and the city where I did my early trading business. Surrounded by generations of family and full of the Bulgarian tradition of which my father is so proud, it was the perfect finale.

What does "Tatko" mean? In Bulgarian it means simply "father." To me, however, it means indescribably more ... my best friend, my

MY SUPPORT GROUP

Fil, Alexandra, Steve and Veronique Filipov at Steve and Alexandra's wedding in Paris, May 1999.

buddy, my mentor. Tatko, thanks for all the guidance and help. I love you.

By the time you read this, there will be another name for him, "Diado." That's Bulgarian for grandfather, that our daughter Astrid will call him soon.

WHAT OTHERS SAY...

Gabor Sztamenits
The Hungarian Refugee and Steve Filipov's
Spiritual Father
Fort Worth, Texas USA
(My notes upon meeting Fil Filipov in 1983, Paris, France)
Aggressive with positive attitude, determined, disciplined, decisive, simple and effective. The basic ingredients of enormous success. He is the most successful Bulgarian product to emerge in the past 50 years.

XI
SOFIA, BULGARIA REVISITED

Just as the business world has experienced major and accelerating change, so has the land of my birth. Stuart Anderson, acknowledged lifting industry spokesperson and consultant, returned to Sofia, Bulgaria's capital city, 25 years later and contributed his impressions of progress made in its culture and economy. They further substantiate "nothing is forever" (nishto ne e vechno) on a grander scale. I wish to express my appreciation to him for this and the *Ode to Filipov* he penned at the time of my 50th birthday which, hopefully, will provide further insight into what I am and where I came from.

SOFIA : 25 YEARS ON

Few, if any, capital cities bear names which have become more widely associated with a person than with the metropolis in question. But such is the fate of Sofia. As my plane descended through the scattered cloud cover above the Bulgarian capital, I wondered if the past quarter century had been as kind to it, as it has, no doubt, to the divine Miss Loren.

Most memories fade with time, others metamorphosize. My recollections of Bulgaria were few but vivid. Driving south from Romania in the depth of winter, a colleague and I had spent two hours being frisked and interrogated by the stern border militia.

Our bright yellow company Range Rover always drew attention and whilst we had "paid-off" the corrupt police with the obligatory Johnny Walker and Marlboros, they had still been particularly unfriendly. By the time we were allowed to proceed, night had fallen and the further we got into the country the deeper the snowdrifts became. After a few kilometers we couldn't see above the snow banked high along each side of the increasingly narrow road. Other than a couple of old trucks and one gypsy riding a horse drawn cart, we didn't see a soul. Three hours later we arrived at the outskirts of our destination – the romantically sounding, but grimy town of Stara Zagora. It was nearly midnight.

It had become quite foggy and the only illumination came from a few old streetlights. While the signs on the highway had been in both English and Cyrillic script, the local road signs were only in the local language, which neither of us could read. Slowly, we navigated the empty streets, peering through the swirling snow for some clue to the location of our hotel. The only sound penetrating the silence was that of our large off-road tyres crunching through the fresh, dense snow. Tired and hungry, we stopped at the first place we found open – a small pokey cafe, it's faint light barely permeating through the large steamed-up front window. As we entered the place we were hit by a thick pall of pungent, Turkish tobacco smoke that hung like a low cloud over the cafe's dozen or so small round plastic-covered tables. Conversation stopped dead as we walked in. Any idea either of us might have had of making a joke about the smoke was instantly forgotten.

Surprisingly for such a late hour, the place was almost full. Maybe the swarthy-looking workers who were dressed mostly in heavy woolen coats and hats had just got off the late shift. Cautiously, we squeezed our way through the small, crowded room to the only vacant table, sat down and kept to ourselves while we waited for the waitress to come over. Neither of us looked around. It seemed as if all of their eyes were on us – as though we'd come from another planet. We could feel their eyes burning into the backs of our heads. It was only after we'd ordered beer and soup by using our fingers to point at what we wanted, that slowly, the locals returned to their conversation, card playing, eating or drinking. As we were leaving, the waitress helpfully pointed out the directions for us to reach our hotel. That night, we shared the same frigid room, and slept with our clothes on. We left very early the following morning, with no desire to sample the hotel's breakfast, neither one of us caring much if we ever saw Stara Zagora again.

Of the brief time we spent in Sofia, I remembered the enormously wide roads and thoroughfares and the huge concrete monoliths that housed their hordes of government workers and bureaucrats. To be fair, the ministry officials we met were of a more pleasant disposition than their counterparts in Bucharest. Seeing the mighty Alexander Nevsky cathedral again brought back memories of my last visit and being completely overwhelmed by its mysterious, dark atmosphere. I had made the journey to the cathedral alone on the last night we were spending in Bulgaria. Although it was only about 10 minutes walk from the Sheraton Hotel at which we were staying, my colleague had refused to accompany me and told me I was crazy. But I've always found the lure of old churches and cathedrals to be irresistible.

Though it looked much older, the gigantic, domed church had been built as recently as 1878. As its name implies, it was erected as a token of thanks to the Russians who had liberated the Bulgarians after five centuries of rule by the Turks. Inside, it was a huge black, cold space, completely silent except for some distant Gregorian chants drifting eerily through the chilled air. I had wanted to look further into the darkness hoping to catch a glimpse of the choir but decided against it. I recall cautiously looking around to try and see if I was being watched by the local KGB. Perhaps I'd seen too many James Bond movies but as I innocently peered up at the dirty stained glass windows, I expected to see a head peep out from behind one of the cathedrals massive columns. In truth in those days one was always conscious of being watched and followed and it wasn't a good idea to give the secret police any excuse to have a go at you. Back then people, even Western visitors, often disappeared without trace or were found dead in the woods. The memory of those few tense minutes, has stayed with me ever since.

Bulgaria has long been amongst the poorest, least developed countries of Eastern Europe and was the slowest to introduce free market reforms. As our plane taxied in, I wondered how far the country had come. From my first impressions of Sofia Airport, the answer was "Not very far!" It still had the look and feel of an old military airfield but as I exited the plane at least the weather was a pleasant surprise – a balmy 60-65 degrees Fahrenheit (15-18°c).

Immigration, baggage and customs went more smoothly than I'd expected and I entered the Arrivals Hall to find throngs of excited locals, many clutching bouquets. While the men were mainly dressed in heavy winter clothes, especially various forms of leather jacket or anoraks, most of the women were more attractively attired. Here too, the Western uniform of black, black and black dominated women's fashion. The girls were much better looking than I'd remembered – slender and for the most part well groomed with long straight hair. Gone was the heavy make-up and bright red lipstick reminiscent of Russian Revolutionary Posters. And while some of the poorer, older women still wear old-fashioned heavy woolen garments in ugly checkered patterns or shiny blouses in fluorescent shades of lime green or pink, the younger generation wear either tight bell-bottomed pants or short mini skirts. These pretty girls were quite a contrast to the squat, heavy-set, swarthy women of my memory. But not all had changed. The men still chain-smoked and police were everywhere. Nevertheless, here at least, the people looked happy and healthy and most were exhibiting a greater pride in their appearance than is often the case in parts of the United States and Western Europe.

Private cars are still not allowed to drive up to the front of the arrivals hall – a security hangover from the old days. But just a short walk away stood a long line of bright yellow taxis and a car park, which though dominated by old Ladas and Trabants also included newish Opels and Fords as well as a few up-market SUVs, Mercedes and BMWs. As we set off from the airport, I noticed that the condition of the main road had improved substantially, with fewer potholes than I'd remembered. However, the standard of driving is still very bad. Many Bulgarian drivers exhibit little lane discipline, constantly meandering all over the road and either undertaking or overtaking at whim. Unleaded gasoline and regular oil changes are also things of the future for the Bulgarian motorist. But maybe breathing in these toxic exhaust fumes is only marginally more harmful than smoking the strongest cigarettes on the planet.

Downtown, mass transit is handled by a variety of dated vehicles. These include long motorbuses with central accordion-like articulating joints, trolley buses and tramcars. All are colorful in their way and offer sporting opportunities that the local motorists gladly accept. Near misses are a way of life on the roads of Sofia. Sparks fly as the trolley buses stretch and bend their masts while the steel wheels of the yellow tramcars screech to the accompaniment of the paced ringing of their bells. It's a comforting happy sound, constant amongst tramcars the world over, as though all of their bells have been struck and tuned to the same chord.

Like in many polluted cities, the skies above Sofia are gray. Indeed much of Sofia is gray. Not that it's a highly industrialized city, far from it. But what industry there is, is heavy, often metallurgical or chemical. And all auto and industrial emissions seem to rise unfiltered into the atmosphere. The grayness of the concrete construction, especially the forests of aging tower blocks, also contributes to the dull image. The ground around these tower blocks is almost always derelict or littered with garbage and there are numerous deserted old buildings and abandoned half-finished construction projects. Dust is everywhere, years of it. It's as though the whole city needs a thorough wash, a torrential downpour to wash away the grime. Certainly the somewhat dry climate contributes to the dust but that isn't the root cause. Indeed the downtown parliamentary area is kept remarkably clean. No, it has to be down to 50 years of public ownership probably reinforced by centuries of foreign rule that's created this apathy towards the urban environment, which only now may be changing.

Apparently, there's a housing shortage in Sofia, but there's little sign of new construction. The tower blocks cheaply thrown-up during the 1950s and 1960s, resplendent with washing drying from every balcony, are now showing their age. Some have already been abandoned. Others look only partially occupied. All look dilapidated. The luckier residents live in the older single-family houses of the suburbs. Yet, despite the ugly apartment building of the Communist era, the city has retained much of its character. It is one of the most heavily wooded capital cities anywhere. One doesn't have to wander very far from the downtown area to find quiet tree-lined avenues with old plaster and timber houses built maybe a hundred years ago. Here one finds a little more color in the faded shades of yellow ocher, pink, rust and sky blue of the plastered walls. These houses were built with pride, love and craftsmanship and although they're quite small and built close together, they almost all have small, cultivated gardens. Here flowers and tomatoes are reared, footpaths swept, woodwork re-painted. Their cozy covered porches, ornamental masonry and carvings, terracotta tiled roofs and warm-colored walls create an individuality and pride that the now-rejected Socialist regime mistakenly dismissed as unnecessary distractions.

Sofia remains a beautiful city, though to see it one must look beneath the dust and decay. And even though it's an old city that has flourished for nearly 2,000 years, the expansive layout of the downtown area has a grandeur and scale rarely found even in the centrally planned cities of the Russian "empire". The wide boulevards and thoroughfares offer spectacular perspectives of the city's many fine churches, old palaces, concert halls, museums and administrative buildings.

Sofia has as many parks as Paris or London, even in the city centery. In the fall, poor, old women with brooms and shovels pursue their futile task of attempting to keep the downtown area free of leaves. Slowly and meticulously, they shuffle along, backs now permanently bent, alone in their thoughts and memories. One of the parks is a haven for old men playing chess, each pair, no doubt, to be found in the same place, each day, each week. Every carefully, painfully contemplated move is respectfully watched and scrutinized by large, huddled groups of engrossed on-lookers. Like the protagonists, the bystanders probably returned each day to their exact same locations, standing or sitting in "their" places.

Another park is the site of a large, colorful daily craft market which like all of the parks has its requisite displays of large metallic sculptures – some religious, others literary, all politically correct. Tall mature trees – elm, oak, beach, ash and silver birch – beautify the parks of Sofia which like parks the world over provide a special sanctuary for playing children and young lovers.

Though it has to fight its way through the smog, the late October sun is strong enough to illuminate and transform the trees still heavy with leaves. They glow with that very Russian autumn yellow color that has inspired so many novelists and poets. The autumn here, or at least this one, seems to be a gentler, more measured affair than the fall in the United States. Maybe due to the unseasonably warm temperatures all of the leaves are the same warm, glowing yellow color and none of them seem to be twisted or mangled in any way. There's no crunch underfoot and no oranges, reds, golds or browns – just yellow.

The parking problem is at its worst in the city center. Apparently significant private car ownership was not envisioned in any of the five-year plans of the earlier Socialist administrations and Sofia seems devoid of parking meters, multi-story and underground parking garages. Small side streets are jam-packed with vehicles carelessly parked and the wider main roads are generally double-parked. But no one seems to care. Police cars, mainly old Ladas painted white and blue are everywhere. However, the more favored ranks of the "Polize" drive big new Mercedes and BMWs and can generally be found parked in plum locations near the foyers of the major hotels or in front of parliamentary buildings. Clearly, some things have yet to change. However, they say that it's very safe to be out alone in the city during daylight and early evening – one positive legacy of the harsh disciplines of the recent past. But, I was told, beware of gypsies and pickpockets!

One very encouraging sign, quite literally, of the market-orientation of the Bulgarians is the vast number of roadside vendors who, each day, set up their stalls either individually or in street markets. Possibly it's the gypsy influence or simply the necessity of farmers and craftsmen to cut out the middlemen and make a small profit from the sale of their merchandise. In any event this almost medieval sub-culture is a major influence on urban life in Bulgaria. Unlike their more raucous counterparts of Anglo-Saxon or Latin descent, these vendors generally go about their business quietly and undemonstratively. Probably another hangover of the police state!

The most highly prized locations for stallholders are along the fashionable downtown shopping streets where one can now find stores exhibiting many of the major fashion names of the West – Gucci, Valentino, Channel, etc. Italian influence is prominent in this part of the world. Other favored locations are in the subways under major road intersections – their weather-proofing proving especially attractive to displays of paintings, wood carvings and old, second-hand or foreign books. The stairwells leading down to these cavernous market locations also provide excellent sites for poster advertising. Here one will find high-quality posters produced by Sofia's substantial printing industry, promoting everything from rock concerts to politicians seeking election. Indeed, a thick mat of torn posters that cover the walls of most old buildings and those of the numerous rusted corrugated-iron shelters. However, the image created by this ménage of posters set against the relief of the city's tree-lined streets and grand architecture combined with the mix of ancient and modern, clean and dirty, and the bohemian life style of the street sellers creates an atmosphere often reminiscent of Paris.

One type of poster, however, is unique to this part of the world. For in Bulgaria, it's a custom to memorialize deceased residents by pasting posters on or near their homes or where they died. These are A4 sized and feature small black-and-white photos of the deceased together with some biographical details. I was told that they are often updated for several years after the death, further memorializing the memory of the subject. Often one will find several copies of these posters stuck on the walls, doors and trees of the home or place involved. Unlike the commercial posters, these aren't dirty, torn or half-covered by another. To me, that spoke volumes about the real qualities of these people and how they had survived their oppressive history.

While, predictably, the majority of local paintings, sold roadside, are cheap, brightly colored landscapes or portraits, there is a large market in replicas of religious icons painted either on finished blocks of wood or sometimes on old broken pieces made to look they came from the ruins of a church. Many of these are quite accomplished. However, most of the woodcarvings are rather crude, reflecting a weakness in artisan skills, which can also be found in the poor quality of the masonry, brickwork, and joinery in contemporary building construction. That there is some spending money here cannot be doubted, but the Bulgarians do love to promenade, slowly wandering through the main shopping streets and regularly stopping to talk at length or to sit and drink coffee or beer. Only the cheap shops seem to be doing good business and most shoppers walk around completely empty-handed.

Farmers choose roadside sites away from the heart of the capital to set-up shop. Most prominent, at least in the fall, are the enormous mounds of giant melons. Like piles of cannonballs but often 18 inches in diameter, what must amount to several truckloads of this fruit can be found strewn along the side of 50 feet or more of the road. One can only wonder at the massive pre-dawn labor involved in simply unloading these pale gray-green mounds. Typically alongside the melons one finds heaps of rock-hard cabbages the size of footballs, more modestly sized pumpkins, giant 3-foot-long leeks bundled up with string like so much firewood, piles of large Spanish onions and peppers and string sacks full of potatoes.

Though late in the year, fruit stalls still offer large, though not especially ripe, beef tomatoes together with local apples, russet pears, plums, pomegranates, dates and figs. Flower giving is still a major tradition in Bulgaria, employed under circumstances too numerous to mention. Though there are many flower sellers in the capital, their displays of roses, chrysanthemums and dahlias are puny by Western standards and clearly have not had the benefit of hothouse treatment.

Even with a nationwide unemployment level nearing 15 percent, there are few beggars or vagrants, at least in the capital. Those that exist are old maimed women or blind men playing violins or cellos, or very young gypsy children. When most work lets out at about 5 p.m., the streets come alive but even so, the crowds display old-fashioned courtesies and considerations for fellow citizens. There is a kind of serenity and tolerance about the people, maybe engendered by being downtrodden by successive, oppressive regimes for so many years. It speaks well for the civilization of these people.

And clearly there has been something of a backlash against the years of socialism as displayed by the very obvious welcoming of Western and especially American culture. Whilst the streets of Sofia are thankfully quiet of the blaring music of some Western cities, when one does hear music being played on the street, it's an incongruous mix of traditional Balkan folk and American rock and rap! Like the rest of the world, Coca Cola has been colonizing Bulgaria for many years and its signature red logo has an ubiquitous presence. At night the full impact of US consumer goods marketing is evident. For even though Sofia has relatively few neon signs, those that there are, are almost all promoting U.S. icons. Here the American tobacco industry promotes its products without the restraints or concerns that now influence it elsewhere. Marlboro, Camel and Lucky Strike signs are everywhere.

And McDonald's golden arches dominate key locations all around town including a facility so large it's like a car park with outside seating for several hundred people. In Bulgaria, a visit to McDonald's is quite a treat, something to sit down to and really appreciate. As someone said to me "McDonald's ist good. Verry good!" The choice of cuisine in the capital has broadened substantially. Though McDonald's dominates the foreign eateries, there are also KFCs, Brazilian, Italian, Chinese, Japanese and Mexican restaurants. However, most people still live on more traditional fare. For starters there are several local salads mostly featuring tomatoes, onions, red cabbage, garlic, peppers and yogurt. As for soups there is tomato and several vegetable types including egg-drop varieties. Numerous kinds of local spicy sausage and other pork dishes such as ribs and meatballs are popular. Lamb is available and is served slow roasted or braised. Beef is less plentiful and not especially good. River trout and some Black Sea fish are available in Sofia, but with question marks against standards of refrigeration and hygiene, smoked fish is probably the best choice. For desert, baklava is by far the local favorite.

Like the Russians, the Bulgarians always set up bottles of Coca Cola, Fruit Squashes and mineral water on the dinner table. Their local beer is good, especially Astika and Kamenitza, which are strong pale Pilsner-type lagers. And the country's fast growing wine industry is starting to be recognized. The Cabernets and Pinot Noirs of the Ruse region in the Northeast are amongst their best.

Service orientation is still a relatively new thing in Bulgaria, so while the waiters are pleasant, smiling souls, they are still learning the ropes and the national lack of a sense of urgency is also noticeable here. However, this lethargy should not be mistaken for a general lack of intelligence. The intelligence of these people shines out through their eyes and is in their laughter. One sees a desire, especially amongst the young, to make something better of themselves. Late in the afternoon, the museums and concert halls fill to capacity with students, parents and children alike. And the country's archeologists and museum curators are keenly exploiting the ever more exciting discoveries of Roman and Greek artifacts from the third century and earlier. It's clear that there is a new awareness and appreciation of the country's long and distinguished heritage that seems to have been all but overlooked for centuries.

Out of town, the countryside reflects a mode of agriculture from much earlier times. For although there are a few old Russian tractors, most of the work is done by peasant farmers on foot or with horses pulling plows or harrows. Farm labor pays very poorly which goes some way to explaining why so much apparently fertile land remains fallow. At least in the areas I visited to the east and south of Sofia, the herds of cattle and sheep are quite small. They're tended by men and boys in ragged clothes working in ways reminiscent of ancient times, and much of their labor on the land, such as sowing seed or gathering crops is done by hand and with tools that have changed little over hundreds of years.

As with so many countries, Bulgaria has potential but is in desperate need of inward investment to bring in new machinery, new industries and to modernize what's already there. The government is gradually introducing privatization of industry and farming is also apparently in a transition away from the collectives of the Socialist era. Formerly state-owned businesses can be purchased very cheaply, but there are question marks against the ability of Bulgarian industry to deliver products and services to quality standards demanded in the West. Changes on the land will probably be the slowest – since most agriculture seems to be in the hands of smallholders or peasant farmers with little capital or education. The residents of Sofia represent most of Bulgaria's brightest hopes, but unless opportunities can be created for the relatively young population, the country could experience a brain drain.

While tourism to the country's Black Sea coastal resorts is

well established, elsewhere it remains minimal. The country has a vast reserve of potential tourist attractions. It's highly diversified landscape not only includes the sandy beaches of the Black Sea but several massive high mountain ranges, deep virgin forests, excellent hunting reserves, extensive archeological finds, ancient monasteries and an impressive capital city. New hotels, including a Hilton in Sofia, are being built and these are badly needed. The quality of building workmanship and customer service will need to improve but it will probably need market forces to bring this about. In fact, properly promoted, tourism may offer one of the best opportunities for Bulgaria. But to fully exploit this will likely need imported Western management talent and it's questionable whether the country's government is yet sufficiently market-oriented to recognize this.

It was a very pleasant, soul-satisfying stay, made especially enjoyable by the warmth of the people and the beauty of some of the buildings and countryside. I look forward to my next visit.

EPILOGUE

Live a good and honorable life. Then when you get older and think back, you'll be able to enjoy it a second time.

Most of what I have to say of course, has been overshadowed by the Internet revolution. My predictions for Y2K computer transitions proved correct – one more gimmick from the computer industry! I am still trying to understand the hype of the emerging new dot-com this, E-that, B2B, B2C, B2ME, B2U, WEB movers and shakers.

Profit has become a dirty word!
Assets are no longer important!
Company valuations are strange!
Mega-big is best!
Multi-rich is fast!
Promises are cheap!
Love is in the options!
Life is like a roller coaster!
Trading is on line!
Gambling is all around!
Who knows – I may never understand it, but I did it my way and I am sure that-
Nothing is forever!
Nishto ne e vechno!

FIL FILIPOV: FILOSOPHIES

WHAT OTHERS SAY...

Richard E. Heath, CPA, CVA
Chief Financial Officer, FILCO, LLC
Myrtle Beach, South Carolina USA
Fil is the epitome of the American dream – from immigrant sweeping the factory floor to CEO of a multinational, multi-plant manufacturing enterprise.

Fil's life demonstrates the results of not only working hard but also working smart and focused at the same time. "Filosophies" is a must-read for those with an eye on the top prizes and qualities of life that are America.

Pratt Gasque
FILCO, LLC General Counsel
Myrtle Beach, South Carolina, USA
Fil Filipov is one of those unusual and interesting persons that a lawyer meets over a lifetime of practice. Fil is a man who started out with absolutely no advantages and overcame many obstacles, such as escaping communism, life in a refugee camp, and confronting languages foreign to his. Starting at the bottom, he has worked his way up to the top of American business. Above all, Fil has vision, a good hands-on management style and a tremendous drive to succeed.

APPENDIX

INDUSTRY OBSERVATIONS

Ben Shaw, Editor
INTERNATIONAL CRANES
Wadhurst, East Sussex
United Kingdom

It has always amazed me that if you want to talk to Fil Filipov, you simply pick up the phone and dial his number. No switchboard, no PA, no "Mr Filipov's office, can I help you?" Just Fil. This illustrates perfectly the business mantra that Fil has applied to Terex Lifting: Simple, Available, Cost Effective. There are no lengthy periods on hold, he is virtually always available and you're never kept hanging around – cost effective.

History has yet to tell us whether his revolutionary approach to crane manufacturing and distribution represents the future of the industry but one thing's for certain, it has certainly forced the competition to re-examine the way it does business. In the past 20 years, no one company head has enjoyed the radical success or earned the reputation (or notoriety, depending on your standpoint) of Fil Filipov.

Undoubtedly he has bigger challenges ahead of him, but these will be greeted with open arms. After escaping Communist Bulgaria and arriving in the United States, he has faced nothing but challenges right up to the present day. Whether he will succeed in the future, as he has in the past, only time will tell.

FIL FILIPOV: FILOSOPHIES

Phil Bishop, Editor
CRANES TODAY
Dartford
United Kingdom

In spite of being a leader in his industry, Filipov likes to portray himself as an underdog and outsider, resolutely not part of the establishment. Is this part of the immigrant's mindset, the legacy of his early life?

For an industry journalist such as myself, Filipov's value is that so long as he's around we will never go short of stories nor lack for someone ready to offer a forthright opinion.

Filipov revels in his image as a man who has shaken up the industry, forcing competitors to look to their laurels. His treatment of cranes as just another commodity, tools which can be sold like hammers and spanners, has not endeared him to many in an industry who place a higher value than Filipov on such concepts as after-sale service and residual value. To Filipov, business is a simple matter. Keep it simple, keep the costs down to a minimum, and offer no more than the market needs. It is a strategy that he has executed in the lifting equipment industry with great focus and the result has been the creation, primarily through acquisition, of a company that manufactures the world's most diversified range of lifting equipment. But is it just house of cards? Terex Lifting is a company built on borrowings that is racing to the stage where it has enough income streams to withstand any market downturns. For all its financial success to date, the Terex story is far from over and there is still much to be done to secure the future health of the company. And there are many in the industry who would feel a warm glow of schadenfreude should the whole edifice collapse. If anyone can prevent that, it is Filipov, aided by Terex Chief Executive Officer Ron DeFeo.

To some, Filipov is ruthless. He would say that you have to be to turn around ailing businesses. There has been, of course, a personal cost

APPENDIX

to the efficiencies that he has brought to bear on acquired companies, with jobs being lost. But in most cases this has been preferable to the alternative – all jobs lost. He may make his employees work hard, but none of them put in the hours that Filipov himself does.

Tim Whiteman, Publishing Editor
The Vertikal Press
Brighton, United Kingdom
If I had a $100 bill for every time somebody said to me of Fil's Terex Lifting, "It just cannot last," I would have at least enough for one of those budget price cranes with which he has revolutionised the crane industry.

So how does he do it? How does he keep all those balls in the air and add another one whenever you think he must be slowing down? How does he keep the money flowing? Since the first time I interviewed him in a Las Vegas hotel about that first, extraordinary purchase of PPM, I have struggled to find the answer.

Friends and enemies alike have all predicted his downfall so many times but he, and Terex, are still here. The impact has been a complete re-appraisal by this traditional and conservative industry of how people buy and make cranes.

"Filosophies" will, I hope, tell me how he keeps all those balls in the air and is bound to be a good read.

FIL FILIPOV: FILOSOPHIES

(Reprinted with permission from the March 1998 issue of Rental Equipment Register. Copyright Intertec Publishing, a PRIMEDIA company.)

MANUFACTURERS' OUTLOOK
Fil Filipov President/CEO Terex Lifting Conway, S.C.

LOWER COSTS AND SIMPLIFIED PRODUCTS WILL LEAD THE WAY

A number of the promising management approaches of the past two decades are failing. Worldwide competitive pressures are slicing margins razor thin.

While adjustments that stem from a global economy ruled by exchange rates will have the most powerful impact on business, they will not be the only factors. Good old-fashioned, down-and-dirty competition will force cost reductions. The watchwords in the current climate are elimination of waste and reduction of corporate bureaucracy and unnecessary administration.

Equipment manufacturers cannot tolerate low productivity and high overheads, and expect customers to continue to pay higher prices. Product development will be dedicated to making products simpler and as cost-effective as possible. Simplicity in the product will reduce the need for highly skilled workers and qualified mechanics. Product safety and reliability will be improved by the use of already-existing standard components. High priority in research and development will be given to weight reductions and environmentally cleaner equipment. Manufacturers will simplify machines, making them more user-friendly.

Pricing will continue to be attractive, and short-term rental and leasing of equipment will grow in new applications, as long as rental rates are reasonable and affordable. As the cost of ownership is discouraged by more competitive rates and fully serviced equip-

APPENDIX

ment, the consolidation of small rental companies will create further downward pressure on rental rates. Equipment utilization will improve, creating the need for larger rental fleets.

The debt-to-earnings ratios of most rental companies currently is reaching 3:1 or 4:1 and will require operating margins of more than 15 percent, which will further increase the drive for higher sales.

The current annual revenues of the rental equipment industry are estimated at about $18 billion to $20 billion, utilizing about $30 billion worth of equipment, 25 percent of which is in the hands of about 10 rental companies.

It is noteworthy that most current rentals and leasing are coming from the petrochemical and non-residential construction industries. The future growth of 10 percent to 15 percent a year will have to come from residential construction and manufacturing companies that currently own their own equipment with an estimated average age of eight to 10 years.

More and more used equipment will be exported to developing countries. Capital needed to renew and grow rental fleets will come from newly discovered financial markets.

As prices and rental rates continue to go down, we can no longer turn our backs to day-to-day operations or seek more sophisticated packaging, larger sales staff, gentler methods or politically correct rules. We will all have to sidestep much of the current methodologies for success and take a more realistic look at the way we are running our businesses. What was great yesterday will not be good enough tomorrow.

As in many other industries, distribution means will continue to evolve. We will see more and more national accounts and non-exclusive distributors competing for the same customers. These users will not be satisfied with the so-called alliances or long-term relationships of the past and will shop around, thus keeping all of us on our toes.

In the past, during periods when the economy and the industries were healthy, the accepted natural reaction was to increase prices. This will not be the case in the coming years, therefore creating opportunities for the lowest-cost producers that will continue to grow their market shares; for the leasing companies that will see improvements in their return on invested capital; and for the user who will continue to enjoy reasonable rates.

ACTION PLAN – FIRST 100 DAYS

(Your Company)

**Action Plan
100 Days
Pain for Gain**

8 M,s

- Manpower
- Machines
- Material
- Markets
- Money
- Morale
- Motivation
- Management

Mission Statement
(Put your company mission statement here)

Action Plan – First 100 Days

■ Manpower

Responsible

1. Headcount – current status and future requirements..........
2. Reporting and approval of all travel in advance..........
3. Productivity and efficiencies measurements and improvements..........
4. Eliminate all consulting and outside service agreements..........
5. Fully absorbed Mfg. cost-per-hour comparisons last 3 years..........
6. Direct labor standard hours by major model for the last 3 years..........
7. Review all lost time accidents past 3 years..........
8. Review salary, past merit and bonus programs..........
9. Sales agents, outside sales people, list/location/agreements..........
10. Eliminate night shifts..........
11. Review labor contract and grievances..........
12. Review any and all employee agreements..........
13. No communication with the press unless authorized in advance..........
14. Disclose all 'cousin' relationships..........

Action Plan – First 100 Days

■ Machines

	Responsible
15. Machine production schedule (MRP) and lead times by model	_____
16. Base machines cost-per-pound	_____
17. Product rationalization by model	_____
18. Define other products to be added to facility	_____
19. Fork lift, company vehicles and all other equipment rationalization	_____
20. New product and prototype introductions	_____
21. R&D computer systems in use and requirements	_____
22. Existing R&D schedule and outstanding design problems	_____
23. Bill of material review by model – total current part numbers	_____
24. Establish intercompany transfer pricing policy	_____
25. Reroute, remove and dispose of old or unused machine tools	_____
26. New color/decal proposal	_____
27. Used equipment – status and disposal	_____
28. By product line (top 10) warranty corrective actions	_____
29. Identify all trademarks and patents	_____

Action Plan – First 100 Days

■ Material   Responsible

30. Communication to suppliers .... _____
31. Plans for supplier reduction program .... _____
32. Letter to suppliers not to sell repair parts direct .... _____
33. Plans for supplier meeting .... _____
34. Complete physical inventory and cycle counting .... _____
35. Inventory status and plans for reductions .... _____
36. Hospital units and status by unit .... _____
37. Top 50 major components and comparison between companies ..... _____
38. Major component strategy .... _____
39. Machine and parts buy back and consignment agreements review ..... _____
40. Review current paint systems and suppliers .... _____
41. Review standard cost system/overhead percentages .... _____
42. Elimination of blanket purchase orders .... _____
43. Review all long-term supply agreements, if any .... _____
44. Coordinate all printing materials .... _____
45. Define stationary, signs, logos, business cards .... _____
46. Obsolete inventory reserves and plans for disposal .... _____
47. Weldment cost-per-pound comparisons .... _____

Action Plan – First 100 Days

■ Material (cont.)

Responsible

48. Turned small parts comparisons .... _____
49. Piece parts cost-per-pound .... _____
50. PPV analysis and corrective actions .... _____
51. Machine unit costs and hours by model – last 3-year history .... _____
52. Daily review of previous days material receipts and PO's issued .. _____
53. Daily shipments report .... _____
54. Spare parts backorder and backlog .... _____
55. Spare parts review and cost comparisons of pirate suppliers .... _____
56. Request dealers to use <u>ALL OEM</u> parts .... _____
57. Spare parts availability status targets and growth strategy .... _____
58. Parts on-line ordering capability for dealers .... _____
59. Vendor return recovery program .... _____
60. Request in writing for substantial price reductions, ... _____
    90-day payment terms and F.O.B. our factory
61. Incoming material inspection and procedures .... _____
62. No vendor price increases to be accepted – .... _____
    there are alternatives. New approval form

Action Plan – First 100 Days

■ Markets

	Responsible
63. Machine backlog and delivery dates	
64. Review the complete distribution network	
65. Review trade shows	
66. Warranty claims – status, reporting and approvals (last 2 years)	
67. Warranty campaign and reserve analysis	
68. Training – who, where, when, costs, etc.	
69. Service calls and technicians - how many, where, etc. Hot Lines	
70. Market share statistics by model	
71. Review any remanufacturing agreements	
72. Review of safety devices and decals used on equipment	
73. Product reliability review	
74. Technical publications complete review	
75. Sales by model for customer and country for last 3 years	
76. Competitive price analysis and pricing guidelines	
77. Government contract administration and business	
78. Payment terms for orders and current customer advances	
79. Establish long-range planning group	

Action Plan – First 100 Days

Responsible

■ Money

80. All capital expenditures are frozen – must review for approval..........
81. Identify status of all loans or grants from any agency..........
82. Eliminate any outside storage rental locations..........
83. Interface financial reporting with corporate..........
84. Fourth quarter financial forecast..........
85. Plans to eliminate leases..........
86. MIS hard and soft costs and headcount review..........
87. Review guard service..........
88. Review any maintenance contracts on equipment..........
89. Establish opening balance sheet..........
90. Transportation costs analysis and reduction program (incl. FedEx)....
91. Approval of expense reports (use company format)..........
92. Phone expense reduction – mobiles, calling cards..........
93. Identify and eliminate all company credit cards..........
94. Identify and eliminate all direct billings..........
95. Listing of all spending descending dollars for the last 2 years..........
96. Implement monthly formal cost reduction program..........

Action Plan – First 100 Days

■ Money (cont.)

	Responsible
97. Y2K compliance review	
98. Outsourcing at 10% less than current variable cost	
99. Identify all commissions paid to whom, why and how much – last 2 years	
100. Insurance costs - regroup to company (investigate)	
101. Daily cash spending and forecast	
102. Accounts receivable aging review	
103. Accounts payable aging review	
104. Identify all company property assigned to people	
105. Prepaid purchases to suppliers	
106. Computer system and PC review	

Action Plan – First 100 Days

■ Morale   Responsible

107. Special report for company magazine .... _____
108. Review absenteeism and take actions .... _____
109. Review safety, OSHA and EPA issues .... _____
110. Schedule an open house and product demonstrations next year ... _____
111. Upgrade all restroom and cafeteria facilities .... _____
112. Cleaning of offices Tuesdays and Thursdays only .... _____
113. Review all employee parking requirements .... _____

■ Motivation   Responsible

114. Introduce lump sum bonus program .... _____
115. Introduce quarterly performance bonuses .... _____
116. Offer jobs at other company locations .... _____
117. Review performance versus salaries .... _____
118. Conduct quarterly all employee meetings .... _____
119. Post company mission statement .... _____
120. Keep local union councils and elected officials informed .... _____

Action Plan – First 100 Days

■ Management

Responsible

121. ISO 9000 status
122. Facility rationalization
123. Establish Profit Plan for upcoming year
124. Openly and clearly communicate our objectives
125. Quickly finalize the organization structure
126. Set aggressive but realistic goals sales and operations - quarterly
127. Eliminate levels of hierarchy
128. Progress tracking
129. List of all employees with job title, current salary, current bonus or commissions, date of employment and last three years merit increase history

Miscellaneous

- Run the business unit as if you own it
- Remember most meetings are a waste of time
- Housekeeping on a daily and hourly basis
- Everything has a place and everything should be in its place
- Do whatever it takes to make things better today than yesterday
- Don't give up – it is up to you to make things happen
- Keep it simple, available and cost effective
- Work harder, longer and smarter
- Follow up, follow up, follow up

REMEMBER: NOTHING IS FOREVER

FIL FILIPOV: FILOSOPHIES

The Eight M's
by Fil Filipov

Winners drive for results.

Losers count the damages. **Whiners** look for excuses.

Success in business comes from taking focused action.

Manpower: A steady diet of hard work does not kill; it makes me live longer and happier. People will make or break the business. When it comes time to reduce headcount, I make a plea for a more humane handling of downsizing. By keeping a constant eye on headcount, direct versus indirect ratios, productivity, efficiency, outsourcing, cost-per-hour and fringe benefits, you can find the "sweet spot" where the perfect number of employees helps the business perform best.

Money: What is a business in the final analysis? The answer of course is money! Most companies can reduce costs by 30% to 50% by doing a few simple things; refuse to accept price increases and re-evaluate commissions and bonuses. Take control of expense reports, reduce phone charges, reduce part numbers and optimize insurance coverage. We need to remember, (receivables+inventory)-payables = working capital.

Material: Like it or not, good housekeeping is essential for quality and efficiency. Not enough people give credit to the adage "a place for everything and everything in its place". Material is money. Do you have just in time or just in case? How high are your part numbers?

Machines: Finished machines are to be sold. Office machines are to help make the sale. Do not let people sell you things you do not need.

Markets: Practice new methods of broadening the markets. Avoid exclusive distribution. Offer price advantages. Take time to understand market share and what it really means. Look at statistics, observations and ways to diagnose performance in the marketplace. Then get out there and take it away from

FIL FILIPOV: FILOSOPHIES

your competitors. Do whatever it takes. What does the order book look like?

Motivation: What is the bottom line? Business is a web of uncertainty. It's a network of diverse problems and complex interdependencies, which we must manage by continually spinning a revising agenda and by keeping tight control of day-to-day operations. Our people must want to work with us. No bureaucracies help contribute to constant motivation improvements.

Morale: Whether there's a risk involved, a move to make, or a decision that must be made quickly, we must make things happen. Morale often hinges on quickly setting clear objectives to respond to changes in the business environment. Those who believe in you go the extra mile. The rest get in the way.

Management: Nothing makes for success in business like a sense of urgency. Leadership involves breathing, eating and sleeping while creating your own "artificial" deadlines with room to make mistakes. Elegance and executive bearing aside, business is basically a boxing match. When boxing, fans and media love the spectacular blows to the head. But, what really wins the match is a constant jab, jab, jab at the opponent's body.

Some punches will get blocked. Some will miss entirely. But if you take aim at the biggest target you can see, and do your best to pound on it persistently, you will win. Every match may not be a knockout. The match may not be over in the second round, but eventually you will win!

A truly successful business in this global environment cannot stand still for a lot of formal theories, empowered networking and consciousness-raising long meetings. While you are trying to get your act together and embrace some new theory, your competitors are punching you where it hurts. In order to be successful, you have to stay in the ring and keep punching day in and day out.

RE-ORDER FORM

Filco LLC will donate profits from this book to Bulgarian Charity Organisations.

I would like to purchase ____ copies of Filosophies

PRICE: GB £11.99 or US $17.99 plus GB £4.95 or US $6.95 P&P

Name

Company

Address

City

Zip/Postcode   County

COUNTRY

Telephone   Fax

Email

Total Value of Order:

☐ I enclose a cheque drawn on a UK bank and made payable to KHLI Services

☐ Please debit my credit card: ☐ Amex   ☐ Diners Club
                                 ☐ Mastercard ☐ Visa

Card No.   Expiry date

Signature

☐ Please invoice me (Book despatched upon payment)

Alternatively:
Purchase the book from KHL's online bookshop – www.khl-bookshop.com
OR telephone the Credit Card sales hotline on +44 (0)1892 784083
OR email bookshop@khl.com with quantity, delivery and payment details.

FIL FILIPOV: FILOSOPHIES